The Clash of Civilizations?
The Debate

Second Edition

FOREIGN
AFFAIRS

Contents

Foreword by
James F. Hoge, Jr.

When the Cold War suddenly ended at the beginning of the 1990s, two critical questions preoccupied international affairs experts: What would be the nature of world politics and the source of conflict in this new world? The most notable analysis was conceived by renowned Harvard professor Samuel P. Huntington.

In "The Clash of Civilizations?" published by *Foreign Affairs* in 1993, Huntington argued that ideological and economic factors would no longer be the fundamental source of conflict. Instead, the great divisions among peoples and nations would be cultural. Thus the principal conflicts of global politics would occur between nations and groups of civilizations that are "differentiated from each other by history, language, culture, tradition and, most important, religion." Since "civilization identity" will be increasingly important, Huntington predicted that "the world will be shaped in large measure by the interactions among seven or eight major civilizations. These include Western, Confucian, Japanese, Islamic, Hindu, Slavic-Orthodox, Latin American and possibly African."

Huntington's striking thesis that the clash of civilizations would dominate global politics was showcased in media around the world and prompted voluminous favorable and critical commentary. To this day, his essay is the most requested reprint from *Foreign Affairs*. Because of the sustained high interest, *Foreign Affairs* published a reader consisting of "The Clash of Civilizations?," commentary from seven well-known experts, and a response from Huntington. Among the commentators' observations were these: conflicts are most likely to break out between nations and groups within a civilization; the enduring nature of citizenship is national; civilizations are

Foreword

absorptive sponges rather than clashing billiard balls; fears of fundamentalist movements are exaggerated and the tenacity of modernity and secularism within civilizations are underestimated; and contrary to realist predictions, most states are not perpetually at war with each other. In response, Huntington documented contemporary examples of the forces that make for clashes between civilizations and argued that they "can be contained only if they are recognized." Whether one subscribes to Huntington's overall thesis, there has been ample evidence in the seventeen years since his landmark essay to support many of his insights.

Foreign Affairs is pleased to present this second edition, in both print and digital format, which features those aforementioned essays as well as three more recent ones.

The Clash of Civilizations?

Samuel P. Huntington

SUMMER 1993

THE NEXT PATTERN OF CONFLICT

World politics is entering a new phase, and intellectuals have not hesitated to proliferate visions of what it will be—the end of history, the return of traditional rivalries between nation states, and the decline of the nation state from the conflicting pulls of tribalism and globalism, among others. Each of these visions catches aspects of the emerging reality. Yet they all miss a crucial, indeed a central, aspect of what global politics is likely to be in the coming years.

It is my hypothesis that the fundamental source of conflict in this new world will not be primarily ideological or primarily economic. The great divisions among humankind and the dominating source of conflict will be cultural. Nation states will remain the most powerful actors in world affairs, but the principal conflicts of global politics will occur between nations and groups of different civilizations. The clash of civilizations will dominate global politics. The fault lines between civilizations will be the battle lines of the future.

Conflict between civilizations will be the latest phase in the

SAMUEL P. HUNTINGTON is the Eaton Professor of the Science of Government and Director of the John M. Olin Institute for Strategic Studies at Harvard University. This article is the product of the Olin Institute's project on "The Changing Security Environment and American National Interests."

evolution of conflict in the modern world. For a century and a half after the emergence of the modern international system with the Peace of Westphalia, the conflicts of the Western world were largely among princes—emperors, absolute monarchs and constitutional monarchs attempting to expand their bureaucracies, their armies, their mercantilist economic strength and, most important, the territory they ruled. In the process they created nation states, and beginning with the French Revolution the principal lines of conflict were between nations rather than princes. In 1793, as R. R. Palmer put it, "The wars of kings were over; the wars of peoples had begun." This nineteenth-century pattern lasted until the end of World War I. Then, as a result of the Russian Revolution and the reaction against it, the conflict of nations yielded to the conflict of ideologies, first among communism, fascism-Nazism and liberal democracy, and then between communism and liberal democracy. During the Cold War, this latter conflict became embodied in the struggle between the two superpowers, neither of which was a nation state in the classical European sense and each of which defined its identity in terms of its ideology.

These conflicts between princes, nation states and ideologies were primarily conflicts within Western civilization, "Western civil wars," as William Lind has labeled them. This was as true of the Cold War as it was of the world wars and the earlier wars of the seventeenth, eighteenth and nineteenth centuries. With the end of the Cold War, international politics moves out of its Western phase, and its centerpiece becomes the interaction between the West and non-Western civilizations and among non-Western civilizations. In the politics of civilizations, the peoples and governments of non-Western civilizations no longer remain the objects of history as targets of Western colonialism but join the West as movers and shapers of history.

Samuel P. Huntington

THE NATURE OF CIVILIZATIONS

During the Cold War the world was divided into the First, Second and Third Worlds. Those divisions are no longer relevant. It is far more meaningful now to group countries not in terms of their political or economic systems or in terms of their level of economic development but rather in terms of their culture and civilization.

What do we mean when we talk of a civilization? A civilization is a cultural entity. Villages, regions, ethnic groups, nationalities, religious groups, all have distinct cultures at different levels of cultural heterogeneity. The culture of a village in southern Italy may be different from that of a village in northern Italy, but both will share in a common Italian culture that distinguishes them from German villages. European communities, in turn, will share cultural features that distinguish them from Arab or Chinese communities. Arabs, Chinese and Westerners, however, are not part of any broader cultural entity. They constitute civilizations. A civilization is thus the highest cultural grouping of people and the broadest level of cultural identity people have short of that which distinguishes humans from other species. It is defined both by common objective elements, such as language, history, religion, customs, institutions, and by the subjective self-identification of people. People have levels of identity: a resident of Rome may define himself with varying degrees of intensity as a Roman, an Italian, a Catholic, a Christian, a European, a Westerner. The civilization to which he belongs is the broadest level of identification with which he intensely identifies. People can and do redefine their identities and, as a result, the composition and boundaries of civilizations change.

Civilizations may involve a large number of people, as with China ("a civilization pretending to be a state," as Lucian Pye put it), or a very small number of people, such as the Anglophone Caribbean. A civilization may include several nation states, as is the case with Western, Latin American and Arab civilizations, or only one, as is the case with Japanese civilization. Civilizations obviously blend and overlap, and may include subcivilizations. Western civilization has two major variants, European and North American, and Islam has its Arab, Turkic and Malay subdivisions. Civilizations are nonetheless meaningful entities, and while the lines between them are seldom sharp, they are real. Civilizations are dynamic; they rise and fall; they divide and merge. And, as any student of history knows, civilizations disappear and are buried in the sands of time.

Westerners tend to think of nation states as the principal actors in global affairs. They have been that, however, for only a few centuries. The broader reaches of human history have been the history of civilizations. In *A Study of History*, Arnold Toynbee identified 21 major civilizations; only six of them exist in the contemporary world.

WHY CIVILIZATIONS WILL CLASH

Civilization identity will be increasingly important in the future, and the world will be shaped in large measure by the interactions among seven or eight major civilizations. These include Western, Confucian, Japanese, Islamic, Hindu, Slavic-Orthodox, Latin American and possibly African civilization. The most important conflicts of the future will occur along the cultural fault lines separating these civilizations from one another.

Why will this be the case?

First, differences among civilizations are not only real; they are basic. Civilizations are differentiated from each other by history, language, culture, tradition and, most important, religion.

Samuel P. Huntington

The people of different civilizations have different views on the relations between God and man, the individual and the group, the citizen and the state, parents and children, husband and wife, as well as differing views of the relative importance of rights and responsibilities, liberty and authority, equality and hierarchy. These differences are the product of centuries. They will not soon disappear. They are far more fundamental than differences among political ideologies and political regimes. Differences do not necessarily mean conflict, and conflict does not necessarily mean violence. Over the centuries, however, differences among civilizations have generated the most prolonged and the most violent conflicts.

Second, the world is becoming a smaller place. The interactions between peoples of different civilizations are increasing; these increasing interactions intensify civilization consciousness and awareness of differences between civilizations and commonalities within civilizations. North African immigration to France generates hostility among Frenchmen and at the same time increased receptivity to immigration by "good" European Catholic Poles. Americans react far more negatively to Japanese investment than to larger investments from Canada and European countries. Similarly, as Donald Horowitz has pointed out, "An Ibo may be . . . an Owerri Ibo or an Onitsha Ibo in what was the Eastern region of Nigeria. In Lagos, he is simply an Ibo. In London, he is a Nigerian. In New York, he is an African." The interactions among peoples of different civilizations enhance the civilization-consciousness of people that, in turn, invigorates differences and animosities stretching or thought to stretch back deep into history.

Third, the processes of economic modernization and social change throughout the world are separating people from longstanding local identities. They also weaken the nation state as a source of identity. In much of the world religion has moved in to fill this gap, often in the form of movements that are labeled "fundamentalist." Such movements are found in Western Christianity, Judaism, Buddhism, and Hinduism, as well as in Islam. In most countries and most religions the people active in fundamentalist movements are young, college-educated, middle-class technicians, professionals and business persons. The "unsecularization of the world," George Weigel has remarked, "is one of the dominant social facts of life in the late twentieth century." The revival of religion, "la revanche de Dieu," as Gilles Kepel labeled it, provides a basis for identity and commitment that transcends national boundaries and unites civilizations.

Fourth, the growth of civilization-consciousness is enhanced by the dual role of the West. On the one hand, the West is at a peak of power. At the same time, however, and perhaps as a result, a return to the roots phenomenon is occurring among non-Western civilizations. Increasingly one hears references to trends toward a turning inward and "Asianization" in Japan, the end of the Nehru legacy and the "Hinduization" of India, the failure of Western ideas of socialism and nationalism and hence "re-Islamization" of the Middle East, and now a debate over Westernization versus Russianization in Boris Yeltsin's country. A West at the peak of its power confronts non-Wests that increasingly have the desire, the will and the resources to shape the world in non-Western ways.

In the past, the elites of non-Western societies were usually the people who were most involved with the West, had been educated at Oxford, the Sorbonne or Sandhurst, and had absorbed Western attitudes and values. At the same time, the populace in non-Western countries often remained deeply imbued with the indigenous culture. Now, however, these relationships are being reversed. A de-Westernization and indigenization of elites is occurring in many non-Western countries at the same time that Western, usually American, cultures, styles, and habits become more popular among the mass of the people.

Fifth, cultural characteristics and differences are less mutable and hence less easily compromised and resolved than political and economic ones. In the former Soviet Union, communists can become democrats, the rich can become poor and the poor rich, but Russians cannot become Estonians and Azeris cannot become Armenians. In class and ideological conflicts, the key question was "Which side are you on?" and people could and did choose sides and change sides. In conflicts between civilizations, the question is "What are you?" That is a given that cannot be changed. And as we know, from Bosnia to the Caucasus to the Sudan, the wrong answer to that question can mean a bullet in the head. Even more than ethnicity, religion discriminates sharply and exclusively among people. A person can be half-French and half-Arab and simultaneously even a citizen of two countries. It is more difficult to be half-Catholic and half-Muslim.

Finally, economic regionalism is increasing. The proportions of total trade that were intraregional rose between 1980 and 1989 from 51 percent to 59 percent in Europe, 33 percent to 37 percent in East Asia, and 32 percent to 36 percent in North America. The importance of regional economic blocs is likely to continue to increase in the future. On the one hand, successful economic regionalism will reinforce civilization-consciousness. On the other hand, economic regionalism may succeed only when it is rooted in a common civilization. The European Community rests on the shared foundation of European culture and Western Christianity. The success of the North American Free Trade Area depends on the convergence now underway of Mexican, Canadian and American cultures. Japan, in contrast, faces difficulties in creating a comparable economic entity in East Asia because Japan is a society and civilization unique to itself. However strong the trade and investment links Japan may develop with other East Asian countries, its cultural differences with those countries inhibit and perhaps preclude its promoting regional economic integration like that in Europe and North America.

Common culture, in contrast, is clearly facilitating the rapid expansion of the economic relations between the People's Republic of China and Hong Kong, Taiwan, Singapore and the overseas Chinese communities in other Asian countries. With the Cold War over, cultural commonalities increasingly overcome ideological differences, and mainland China and Taiwan move closer together. If cultural commonality is a prerequisite for economic integration, the principal East Asian economic bloc of the future is likely to be centered on China. This bloc is, in fact, already coming into existence. As Murray Weidenbaum has observed,

> Despite the current Japanese dominance of the region, the Chinese-based economy of Asia is rapidly emerging as a new epicenter for industry, commerce and finance. This strategic area contains substantial amounts of technology and manufacturing capability (Taiwan), outstanding entrepreneurial, marketing and services acumen (Hong Kong), a fine communications network (Singapore), a tremendous pool of financial capital (all three), and very large endowments of land, resources and labor (mainland China). . . . From Guangzhou to Singapore, from Kuala Lumpur to Manila, this influential network—often based on extensions of the traditional clans—has been described as the backbone of the East Asian economy.[1]

Culture and religion also form the basis of the Economic Cooperation Organization, which brings together ten non-Arab Muslim countries: Iran, Pakistan, Turkey, Azerbaijan, Kazakhstan, Kyrgyzstan, Turkmenistan, Tadjikistan, Uzbekistan and Afghanistan. One impetus to the revival and expansion of this organization, founded originally in the 1960s by Turkey, Pakistan and Iran, is the realization by the leaders of several of these countries that they had no chance of admission to the European Community. Similarly, Caricom, the Central

---

[1]Murray Weidenbaum, *Greater China: The Next Economic Superpower?*, St. Louis: Washington University Center for the Study of American Business, Contemporary Issues, Series 57, February 1993, pp. 2–3.

American Common Market and Mercosur rest on common cultural foundations. Efforts to build a broader Caribbean-Central American economic entity bridging the Anglo-Latin divide, however, have to date failed.

As people define their identity in ethnic and religious terms, they are likely to see an "us" versus "them" relation existing between themselves and people of different ethnicity or religion. The end of ideologically defined states in Eastern Europe and the former Soviet Union permits traditional ethnic identities and animosities to come to the fore. Differences in culture and religion create differences over policy issues, ranging from human rights to immigration to trade and commerce to the environment. Geographical propinquity gives rise to conflicting territorial claims from Bosnia to Mindanao. Most important, the efforts of the West to promote its values of democracy and liberalism as universal values, to maintain its military predominance and to advance its economic interests engender countering responses from other civilizations. Decreasingly able to mobilize support and form coalitions on the basis of ideology, governments and groups will increasingly attempt to mobilize support by appealing to common religion and civilization identity.

The clash of civilizations thus occurs at two levels. At the microlevel, adjacent groups along the fault lines between civilizations struggle, often violently, over the control of territory and each other. At the macro-level, states from different civilizations compete for relative military and economic power, struggle over the control of international institutions and third parties, and competitively promote their particular political and religious values.

THE FAULT LINES BETWEEN CIVILIZATIONS

The fault lines between civilizations are replacing the political and ideological boundaries of the Cold War as the flash points for crisis and bloodshed. The Cold War began when the Iron Curtain divided Europe politically and ideologically. The Cold War ended with the end of the Iron Curtain. As the ideological division of Europe has disappeared, the cultural division of Europe between Western Christianity, on the one hand, and Orthodox Christianity and Islam, on the other, has reemerged. The most significant dividing line in Europe, as William Wallace has suggested, may well be the eastern boundary of Western Christianity in the year 1500. This line runs along what are now the boundaries between Finland and Russia and between the Baltic states and Russia, cuts through Belarus and Ukraine separating the more Catholic western Ukraine from Orthodox eastern Ukraine, swings westward separating Transylvania from the rest of Romania, and then goes through Yugoslavia almost exactly along the line now separating Croatia and Slovenia from the rest of Yugoslavia. In the Balkans this line, of course, coincides with the historic boundary between the Hapsburg and Ottoman empires. The peoples to the north and west of this line are Protestant or Catholic; they shared the common experiences of European history—feudalism, the Renaissance, the Reformation, the Enlightenment, the French Revolution, the Industrial Revolution; they are generally economically better off than the peoples to the east; and they may now look forward to increasing involvement in a common European economy and to the consolidation of democratic political systems. The peoples to the east and south of this line are Orthodox or Muslim; they historically belonged to the Ottoman or Tsarist empires and were only lightly touched by the shaping events in the rest of Europe; they are generally less advanced economically; they seem much less likely to develop stable democratic political systems. The Velvet Curtain of culture has replaced the Iron Curtain of ideology as the most significant dividing line in Europe. As the events in Yugoslavia show, it is not only a line of difference; it is also at times a line of bloody conflict.

Conflict along the fault line between Western and Islamic civilizations has been going on for 1,300 years. After the founding of Islam, the Arab and Moorish surge west and north only ended at Tours in 732. From the eleventh to the thirteenth century the Crusaders attempted with temporary success to bring Christianity and Christian rule to the Holy Land. From the fourteenth to the seventeenth century, the Ottoman Turks reversed the balance, extended their sway over the Middle East and the Balkans, captured Constantinople, and twice laid siege to Vienna. In the nineteenth and early twentieth centuries as Ottoman power declined Britain, France, and Italy established Western control over most of North Africa and the Middle East.

After World War II, the West, in turn, began to retreat; the colonial empires disappeared; first Arab nationalism and then Islamic fundamentalism manifested themselves; the West became heavily dependent on the Persian Gulf countries for its energy; the oil-rich Muslim countries became money-rich and, when they wished to, weapons-rich. Several wars occurred between Arabs and Israel (created by the West). France fought a bloody and ruthless war in Algeria for most of the 1950s; British and French forces invaded Egypt in 1956; American forces went into Lebanon in 1958; subsequently American forces returned to Lebanon, attacked Libya, and engaged in various military encounters with Iran; Arab and Islamic terrorists, supported by at least three Middle Eastern governments, employed the weapon of the weak and bombed Western planes and installations and seized Western hostages. This warfare between Arabs and the West culminated in 1990, when the United States sent a massive army to the Persian Gulf to defend some Arab countries against aggression by another. In its aftermath NATO planning is increasingly directed to potential threats and instability along its "southern tier."

This centuries-old military interaction between the West and Islam is unlikely to decline. It could become more virulent. The Gulf War left some Arabs feeling proud that Saddam Hussein had attacked Israel and stood up to the West. It also left many feeling humiliated and resentful of the West's military presence in the Persian Gulf, the West's overwhelming military dominance, and their apparent inability to shape their own destiny. Many Arab countries, in addition to the oil exporters, are reaching levels of economic and social development where autocratic forms of government become inappropriate and efforts to introduce democracy become stronger. Some openings in Arab political systems have already occurred. The principal beneficiaries of these openings have been Islamist movements. In the Arab world, in short, Western democracy strengthens anti-Western political forces. This may be a passing phenomenon, but it surely complicates relations between Islamic countries and the West.

Those relations are also complicated by demography. The spectacular population growth in Arab countries, particularly in North Africa, has led to increased migration to Western Europe. The movement within Western Europe toward minimizing internal boundaries has sharpened political sensitivities with respect to this development. In Italy, France and Germany, racism is increasingly open, and political reactions and violence against Arab and Turkish migrants have become more intense and more widespread since 1990.

On both sides the interaction between Islam and the West is seen as a clash of civilizations. The West's "next confrontation," observes M. J. Akbar, an Indian Muslim author, "is definitely going to come from the Muslim world. It is in the sweep of the Islamic nations from the Maghreb to Pakistan that the struggle for a new world order will begin." Bernard Lewis comes to a similar conclusion:

Samuel P. Huntington

We are facing a mood and a movement far transcending the level of issues and policies and the governments that pursue them. This is no less than a clash of civilizations—the perhaps irrational but surely historic reaction of an ancient rival against our Judeo-Christian heritage, our secular present, and the world-wide expansion of both.[2]

Historically, the other great antagonistic interaction of Arab Islamic civilization has been with the pagan, animist, and now increasingly Christian black peoples to the south. In the past, this antagonism was epitomized in the image of Arab slave dealers and black slaves. It has been reflected in the on-going civil war in the Sudan between Arabs and blacks, the fighting in Chad between Libyan-supported insurgents and the government, the tensions between Orthodox Christians and Muslims in the Horn of Africa, and the political conflicts, recurring riots and communal violence between Muslims and Christians in Nigeria. The modernization of Africa and the spread of Christianity are likely to enhance the probability of violence along this fault line. Symptomatic of the intensification of this conflict was the Pope John Paul II's speech in Khartoum in February 1993 attacking the actions of the Sudan's Islamist government against the Christian minority there.

On the northern border of Islam, conflict has increasingly erupted between Orthodox and Muslim peoples, including the carnage of Bosnia and Sarajevo, the simmering violence between Serb and Albanian, the tenuous relations between Bulgarians and their Turkish minority, the violence between Ossetians and Ingush, the unremitting slaughter of each other by Armenians and Azeris, the tense relations between Russians and Muslims in Central Asia, and the deployment of Russian troops to protect Russian interests in the Caucasus and Central Asia. Religion reinforces the revival of ethnic identities and

---

[2]Bernard Lewis, "The Roots of Muslim Rage," *The Atlantic Monthly*, vol. 266, September 1990, p. 60; *Time*, June 15, 1992, pp. 24–28.

restimulates Russian fears about the security of their southern borders. This concern is well captured by Archie Roosevelt:

> Much of Russian history concerns the struggle between the Slavs and the Turkic peoples on their borders, which dates back to the foundation of the Russian state more than a thousand years ago. In the Slavs' millennium-long confrontation with their eastern neighbors lies the key to an understanding not only of Russian history, but Russian character. To understand Russian realities today one has to have a concept of the great Turkic ethnic group that has preoccupied Russians through the centuries.[3]

The conflict of civilizations is deeply rooted elsewhere in Asia. The historic clash between Muslim and Hindu in the subcontinent manifests itself now not only in the rivalry between Pakistan and India but also in intensifying religious strife within India between increasingly militant Hindu groups and India's substantial Muslim minority. The destruction of the Ayodhya mosque in December 1992 brought to the fore the issue of whether India will remain a secular democratic state or become a Hindu one. In East Asia, China has outstanding territorial disputes with most of its neighbors. It has pursued a ruthless policy toward the Buddhist people of Tibet, and it is pursuing an increasingly ruthless policy toward its Turkic-Muslim minority. With the Cold War over, the underlying differences between China and the United States have reasserted themselves in areas such as human rights, trade and weapons proliferation. These differences are unlikely to moderate. A "new cold war," Deng Xaioping reportedly asserted in 1991, is under way between China and America.

The same phrase has been applied to the increasingly difficult relations between Japan and the United States. Here cultural difference exacerbates economic conflict. People on each side allege racism on the other, but at least on the American side the antipathies are not racial but cultural. The basic values,

---

[3]Archie Roosevelt, *For Lust of Knowing*, Boston: Little, Brown, 1988, pp. 332–333.

attitudes, behavioral patterns of the two societies could hardly be more different. The economic issues between the United States and Europe are no less serious than those between the United States and Japan, but they do not have the same political salience and emotional intensity because the differences between American culture and European culture are so much less than those between American civilization and Japanese civilization.

The interactions between civilizations vary greatly in the extent to which they are likely to be characterized by violence. Economic competition clearly predominates between the American and European subcivilizations of the West and between both of them and Japan. On the Eurasian continent, however, the proliferation of ethnic conflict, epitomized at the extreme in "ethnic cleansing," has not been totally random. It has been most frequent and most violent between groups belonging to different civilizations. In Eurasia the great historic fault lines between civilizations are once more aflame. This is particularly true along the boundaries of the crescent-shaped Islamic bloc of nations from the bulge of Africa to central Asia. Violence also occurs between Muslims, on the one hand, and Orthodox Serbs in the Balkans, Jews in Israel, Hindus in India, Buddhists in Burma and Catholics in the Philippines. Islam has bloody borders.

CIVILIZATION RALLYING:
THE KIN-COUNTRY SYNDROME

Groups or states belonging to one civilization that become involved in war with people from a different civilization naturally try to rally support from other members of their own civilization. As the post–Cold War world evolves, civilization commonality, what H. D. S. Greenway has termed the "kin-country" syndrome, is replacing political ideology and traditional balance of power considerations as the principal basis for cooperation and coalitions. It can be seen gradually emerging in the post–Cold War conflicts in the Persian Gulf, the Caucasus and Bosnia. None of these was a full-scale war between civilizations, but each involved some elements of civilizational rallying, which seemed to become more important as the conflict continued and which may provide a foretaste of the future.

First, in the Gulf War one Arab state invaded another and then fought a coalition of Arab, Western and other states. While only a few Muslim governments overtly supported Saddam Hussein, many Arab elites privately cheered him on, and he was highly popular among large sections of the Arab publics. Islamic fundamentalist movements universally supported Iraq rather than the Western-backed governments of Kuwait and Saudi Arabia. Forswearing Arab nationalism, Saddam Hussein explicitly invoked an Islamic appeal. He and his supporters attempted to define the war as a war between civilizations. "It is not the world against Iraq," as Safar Al-Hawali, dean of Islamic Studies at the Umm Al-Qura University in Mecca, put it in a widely circulated tape. "It is the West against Islam." Ignoring the rivalry between Iran and Iraq, the chief Iranian religious leader, Ayatollah Ali Khamenei, called for a holy war against the West: "The struggle against American aggression, greed, plans and policies will be counted as a jihad, and anybody who is killed on that path is a martyr." "This is a war," King Hussein of Jordan argued, "against all Arabs and all Muslims and not against Iraq alone."

The rallying of substantial sections of Arab elites and publics behind Saddam Hussein caused those Arab governments in the anti-Iraq coalition to moderate their activities and temper their public statements. Arab governments opposed or distanced themselves from subsequent Western efforts to apply pressure on Iraq, including enforcement of a no-fly zone in the summer of 1992 and the bombing of Iraq in January 1993. The Western-Soviet-Turkish-Arab anti-Iraq coalition of 1990 had by 1993 become a coalition of almost only the West and Kuwait against Iraq.

Muslims contrasted Western actions against Iraq with the West's failure to protect Bosnians against Serbs and to impose sanctions on Israel for violating UN resolutions. The West, they alleged, was using a double standard. A world of clashing civilizations, however, is inevitably a world of double standards: people apply one standard to their kin-countries and a different standard to others.

Second, the kin-country syndrome also appeared in conflicts in the former Soviet Union. Armenian military successes in 1992 and 1993 stimulated Turkey to become increasingly supportive of its religious, ethnic and linguistic brethren in Azerbaijan. "We have a Turkish nation feeling the same sentiments as the Azerbaijanis," said one Turkish official in 1992. "We are under pressure. Our newspapers are full of the photos of atrocities and are asking us if we are still serious about pursuing our neutral policy. Maybe we should show Armenia that there's a big Turkey in the region." President Turgut Özal agreed, remarking that Turkey should at least "scare the Armenians a little bit." Turkey, Özal threatened again in 1993, would "show its fangs." Turkish Air Force jets flew reconnaissance flights along the Armenian border; Turkey suspended food shipments and air flights to Armenia; and Turkey and Iran announced they would not accept dismemberment of Azerbaijan. In the last years of its existence, the Soviet government supported Azerbaijan because its government was dominated by former communists. With the end of the Soviet Union, however, political considerations gave way to religious ones. Russian troops fought on the side of the Armenians, and Azerbaijan accused the "Russian government of turning 180 degrees" toward support for Christian Armenia.

Third, with respect to the fighting in the former Yugoslavia, Western publics manifested sympathy and support for the Bosnian Muslims and the horrors they suffered at the hands of the Serbs. Relatively little concern was expressed, however, over Croatian attacks on Muslims and participation in the dismemberment of Bosnia-Herzegovina. In the early stages of the Yugoslav breakup, Germany, in an unusual display of diplomatic initiative and muscle, induced the other 11 members of the European Community to follow its lead in recognizing Slovenia and Croatia. As a result of the pope's determination to provide strong backing to the two Catholic countries, the Vatican extended recognition even before the Community did. The United States followed the European lead. Thus the leading actors in Western civilization rallied behind their coreligionists. Subsequently Croatia was reported to be receiving substantial quantities of arms from Central European and other Western countries. Boris Yeltsin's government, on the other hand, attempted to pursue a middle course that would be sympathetic to the Orthodox Serbs but not alienate Russia from the West. Russian conservative and nationalist groups, however, including many legislators, attacked the government for not being more forthcoming in its support for the Serbs. By early 1993 several hundred Russians apparently were serving with the Serbian forces, and reports circulated of Russian arms being supplied to Serbia.

Islamic governments and groups, on the other hand, castigated the West for not coming to the defense of the Bosnians. Iranian leaders urged Muslims from all countries to provide help to Bosnia; in violation of the UN arms embargo, Iran supplied weapons and men for the Bosnians; Iranian-supported Lebanese groups sent guerrillas to train and organize the Bosnian forces. In 1993 up to 4,000 Muslims from over two dozen Islamic countries were reported to be fighting in Bosnia. The governments of Saudi Arabia and other countries felt under increasing pressure from fundamentalist groups in their own societies to provide more vigorous support for the Bosnians. By the end of 1992, Saudi Arabia had reportedly supplied substantial funding for weapons and supplies for the Bosnians, which significantly increased their military capabilities vis-à-vis the Serbs.

In the 1930s the Spanish Civil War provoked intervention from countries that politically were fascist, communist and democratic. In the 1990s the Yugoslav conflict is provoking intervention from countries that are Muslim, Orthodox and Western Christian. The parallel has not gone unnoticed. "The war in Bosnia-Herzegovina has become the emotional equivalent of the fight against fascism in the Spanish Civil War," one Saudi editor observed. "Those who died there are regarded as martyrs who tried to save their fellow Muslims."

Conflicts and violence will also occur between states and groups within the same civilization. Such conflicts, however, are likely to be less intense and less likely to expand than conflicts between civilizations. Common membership in a civilization reduces the probability of violence in situations where it might otherwise occur. In 1991 and 1992 many people were alarmed by the possibility of violent conflict between Russia and Ukraine over territory, particularly Crimea, the Black Sea fleet, nuclear weapons and economic issues. If civilization is what counts, however, the likelihood of violence between Ukrainians and Russians should be low. They are two Slavic, primarily Orthodox peoples who have had close relationships with each other for centuries. As of early 1993, despite all the reasons for conflict, the leaders of the two countries were effectively negotiating and defusing the issues between the two countries. While there has been serious fighting between Muslims and Christians elsewhere in the former Soviet Union and much tension and some fighting between Western and Orthodox Christians in the Baltic states, there has been virtually no violence between Russians and Ukrainians.

Civilization rallying to date has been limited, but it has been growing, and it clearly has the potential to spread much further. As the conflicts in the Persian Gulf, the Caucasus and Bosnia continued, the positions of nations and the cleavages between them increasingly were along civilizational lines. Populist politicians, religious leaders and the media have found it a potent means of arousing mass support and of pressuring hesitant governments. In the coming years, the local conflicts most likely to escalate into major wars will be those, as in Bosnia and the Caucasus, along the fault lines between civilizations. The next world war, if there is one, will be a war between civilizations.

THE WEST VERSUS THE REST

The west is now at an extraordinary peak of power in relation to other civilizations. Its superpower opponent has disappeared from the map. Military conflict among Western states is unthinkable, and Western military power is unrivaled. Apart from Japan, the West faces no economic challenge. It dominates international political and security institutions and with Japan international economic institutions. Global political and security issues are effectively settled by a directorate of the United States, Britain and France, world economic issues by a directorate of the United States, Germany and Japan, all of which maintain extraordinarily close relations with each other to the exclusion of lesser and largely non-Western countries. Decisions made at the UN Security Council or in the International Monetary Fund that reflect the interests of the West are presented to the world as reflecting the desires of the world community. The very phrase "the world community" has become the euphemistic collective noun (replacing "the Free World") to give global legitimacy to actions reflecting the interests of the United States and other Western powers.⁴ Through the IMF and other international economic institutions, the West promotes its economic interests and imposes on other nations the economic policies it thinks appropriate. In any poll of non-Western peoples, the IMF undoubtedly would win the support of finance ministers and a few others, but get an overwhelmingly unfavorable rating from just about everyone else, who would agree with Georgy Arbatov's characterization of IMF officials as "neo-Bolsheviks who love expropriating other people's money, imposing undemocratic and alien rules of economic and political conduct and stifling economic freedom."

Western domination of the UN Security Council and its decisions, tempered only by occasional abstention by China, produced UN legitimation of the West's use of force to drive Iraq out of Kuwait and its elimination of Iraq's sophisticated weapons and capacity to produce such weapons. It also produced the quite unprecedented action by the United States, Britain and France in getting the Security Council to demand that Libya hand over the Pan Am 103 bombing suspects and then to impose sanctions when Libya refused. After defeating the largest Arab army, the West did not hesitate to throw its weight around in the Arab world. The West in effect is using international institutions, military power and economic resources to run the world in ways that will maintain Western predominance, protect Western interests and promote Western political and economic values.

That at least is the way in which non-Westerners see the new

---

⁴Almost invariably Western leaders claim they are acting on behalf of "the world community." One minor lapse occurred during the run-up to the Gulf War. In an interview on "Good Morning America," Dec. 21, 1990, British Prime Minister John Major referred to the actions "the West" was taking against Saddam Hussein. He quickly corrected himself and subsequently referred to "the world community." He was, however, right when he erred.

world, and there is a significant element of truth in their view. Differences in power and struggles for military, economic and institutional power are thus one source of conflict between the West and other civilizations. Differences in culture, that is basic values and beliefs, are a second source of conflict. V. S. Naipaul has argued that Western civilization is the "universal civilization" that "fits all men." At a superficial level much of Western culture has indeed permeated the rest of the world. At a more basic level, however, Western concepts differ fundamentally from those prevalent in other civilizations. Western ideas of individualism, liberalism, constitutionalism, human rights, equality, liberty, the rule of law, democracy, free markets, the separation of church and state, often have little resonance in Islamic, Confucian, Japanese, Hindu, Buddhist or Orthodox cultures. Western efforts to propagate such ideas produce instead a reaction against "human rights imperialism" and a reaffirmation of indigenous values, as can be seen in the support for religious fundamentalism by the younger generation in non-Western cultures. The very notion that there could be a "universal civilization" is a Western idea, directly at odds with the particularism of most Asian societies and their emphasis on what distinguishes one people from another. Indeed, the author of a review of 100 comparative studies of values in different societies concluded that "the values that are most important in the West are least important worldwide."[5] In the political realm, of course, these differences are most manifest in the efforts of the United States and other Western powers to induce other peoples to adopt Western ideas concerning democracy and human rights. Modern democratic government originated in the West. When it has developed in non-Western societies it has usually

---

[5]Harry C. Triandis, *The New York Times*, Dec. 25, 1990, p. 41, and "Cross-Cultural Studies of Individualism and Collectivism," Nebraska Symposium on Motivation, vol. 37, 1989, pp. 41–133.

been the product of Western colonialism or imposition.

The central axis of world politics in the future is likely to be, in Kishore Mahbubani's phrase, the conflict between "the West and the Rest" and the responses of non-Western civilizations to Western power and values.[6] Those responses generally take one or a combination of three forms. At one extreme, non-Western states can, like Burma and North Korea, attempt to pursue a course of isolation, to insulate their societies from penetration or "corruption" by the West, and, in effect, to opt out of participation in the Western-dominated global community. The costs of this course, however, are high, and few states have pursued it exclusively. A second alternative, the equivalent of "band-wagoning" in international relations theory, is to attempt to join the West and accept its values and institutions. The third alternative is to attempt to "balance" the West by developing economic and military power and cooperating with other non-Western societies against the West, while preserving indigenous values and institutions; in short, to modernize but not to Westernize.

THE TORN COUNTRIES

In the future, as people differentiate themselves by civilization, countries with large numbers of peoples of different civilizations, such as the Soviet Union and Yugoslavia, are candidates for dismemberment. Some other countries have a fair degree of cultural homogeneity but are divided over whether their society belongs to one civilization or another. These are torn countries. Their leaders typically wish to pursue a bandwagoning strategy and to make their countries members of the West, but the history, culture and traditions of their countries are non-Western.

---

[6]Kishore Mahbubani, "The West and the Rest," *The National Interest*, Summer 1992, pp. 3–13.

The most obvious and prototypical torn country is Turkey. The late twentieth-century leaders of Turkey have followed in the Attatürk tradition and defined Turkey as a modern, secular, Western nation state. They allied Turkey with the West in NATO and in the Gulf War; they applied for membership in the European Community. At the same time, however, elements in Turkish society have supported an Islamic revival and have argued that Turkey is basically a Middle Eastern Muslim society. In addition, while the elite of Turkey has defined Turkey as a Western society, the elite of the West refuses to accept Turkey as such. Turkey will not become a member of the European Community, and the real reason, as President Özal said, "is that we are Muslim and they are Christian and they don't say that." Having rejected Mecca, and then being rejected by Brussels, where does Turkey look? Tashkent may be the answer. The end of the Soviet Union gives Turkey the opportunity to become the leader of a revived Turkic civilization involving seven countries from the borders of Greece to those of China. Encouraged by the West, Turkey is making strenuous efforts to carve out this new identity for itself.

During the past decade Mexico has assumed a position somewhat similar to that of Turkey. Just as Turkey abandoned its historic opposition to Europe and attempted to join Europe, Mexico has stopped defining itself by its opposition to the United States and is instead attempting to imitate the United States and to join it in the North American Free Trade Area. Mexican leaders are engaged in the great task of redefining Mexican identity and have introduced fundamental economic reforms that eventually will lead to fundamental political change. In 1991 a top adviser to President Carlos Salinas de Gortari described at length to me all the changes the Salinas government was making. When he finished, I remarked: "That's most impressive. It seems to me that basically you want to change Mexico from a Latin American country into a North American country." He looked at me with surprise and exclaimed: "Exactly! That's precisely what we are trying to do, but of course we could never say so publicly." As his remark indicates, in Mexico as in Turkey, significant elements in society resist the redefinition of their country's identity. In Turkey, European-oriented leaders have to make gestures to Islam (Özal's pilgrimage to Mecca); so also Mexico's North American-oriented leaders have to make gestures to those who hold Mexico to be a Latin American country (Salinas' Ibero-American Guadalajara summit).

Historically Turkey has been the most profoundly torn country. For the United States, Mexico is the most immediate torn country. Globally the most important torn country is Russia. The question of whether Russia is part of the West or the leader of a distinct Slavic-Orthodox civilization has been a recurring one in Russian history. That issue was obscured by the communist victory in Russia, which imported a Western ideology, adapted it to Russian conditions and then challenged the West in the name of that ideology. The dominance of communism shut off the historic debate over Westernization versus Russification. With communism discredited Russians once again face that question.

President Yeltsin is adopting Western principles and goals and seeking to make Russia a "normal" country and a part of the West. Yet both the Russian elite and the Russian public are divided on this issue. Among the more moderate dissenters, Sergei Stankevich argues that Russia should reject the "Atlanticist" course, which would lead it "to become European, to become a part of the world economy in rapid and organized fashion, to become the eighth member of the Seven, and to put particular emphasis on Germany and the United States as the two dominant members of the Atlantic alliance." While also rejecting an exclusively Eurasian policy, Stankevich nonetheless argues that Russia should give priority to the protection of Russians in other countries, emphasize its Turkic and Muslim connections, and promote "an appreciable redistribution of our resources, our options, our ties, and our interests in favor of Asia, of the eastern direction." People of this persuasion criticize Yeltsin for subordinating Russia's interests to those of the West, for reducing Russian military strength, for failing to support traditional friends such as Serbia, and for pushing economic and political reform in ways injurious to the Russian people. Indicative of this trend is the new popularity of the ideas of Petr Savitsky, who in the 1920s argued that Russia was a unique Eurasian civilization.[7] More extreme dissidents voice much more blatantly nationalist, anti-Western and anti-Semitic views, and urge Russia to redevelop its military strength and to establish closer ties with China and Muslim countries. The people of Russia are as divided as the elite. An opinion survey in European Russia in the spring of 1992 revealed that 40 percent of the public had positive attitudes toward the West and 36 percent had negative attitudes. As it has been for much of its history, Russia in the early 1990s is truly a torn country.

To redefine its civilization identity, a torn country must meet three requirements. First, its political and economic elite has to be generally supportive of and enthusiastic about this move. Second, its public has to be willing to acquiesce in the redefinition. Third, the dominant groups in the recipient civilization have to be willing to embrace the convert. All three requirements in large part exist with respect to Mexico. The first two in large part exist with respect to Turkey. It is not clear that any of them exist with respect to Russia's joining the West. The conflict between liberal democracy and Marxism-Leninism was between ideologies which, despite their major differences, ostensibly shared ultimate goals of freedom, equality

---

[7]Sergei Stankevich, "Russia in Search of Itself," *The National Interest*, Summer 1992, pp. 47–51; Daniel Schneider, "A Russian Movement Rejects Western Tilt," *Christian Science Monitor*, Feb. 5, 1993, pp. 5–7.

and prosperity. A traditional, authoritarian, nationalist Russia could have quite different goals. A Western democrat could carry on an intellectual debate with a Soviet Marxist. It would be virtually impossible for him to do that with a Russian traditionalist. If, as the Russians stop behaving like Marxists, they reject liberal democracy and begin behaving like Russians but not like Westerners, the relations between Russia and the West could again become distant and conflictual.[8]

THE CONFUCIAN-ISLAMIC CONNECTION

The obstacles to non-Western countries joining the West vary considerably. They are least for Latin American and East European countries. They are greater for the Orthodox countries of the former Soviet Union. They are still greater for Muslim, Confucian, Hindu and Buddhist societies. Japan has established a unique position for itself as an associate member of the West: it is in the West in some respects but clearly not of the West in important dimensions. Those countries that for reason of culture and power do not wish to, or cannot, join the West compete with the West by developing their own economic, military and political power. They do this by promoting their internal development and by cooperating with other non-Western countries. The most prominent form of this cooperation is the Confucian-Islamic connection that has emerged to challenge Western interests, values and power.

---

[8]Owen Harries has pointed out that Australia is trying (unwisely in his view) to become a torn country in reverse. Although it has been a full member not only of the West but also of the ABCA military and intelligence core of the West, its current leaders are in effect proposing that it defect from the West, redefine itself as an Asian country and cultivate close ties with its neighbors. Australia's future, they argue, is with the dynamic economies of East Asia. But, as I have suggested, close economic cooperation normally requires a common cultural base. In addition, none of the three conditions necessary for a torn country to join another civilization is likely to exist in Australia's case.

Almost without exception, Western countries are reducing their military power; under Yeltsins leadership so also is Russia. China, North Korea and several Middle Eastern states, however, are significantly expanding their military capabilities. They are doing this by the import of arms from Western and non-Western sources and by the development of indigenous arms industries. One result is the emergence of what Charles Krauthammer has called "Weapon States," and the Weapon States are not Western states. Another result is the redefinition of arms control, which is a Western concept and a Western goal. During the Cold War the primary purpose of arms control was to establish a stable military balance between the United States and its allies and the Soviet Union and its allies. In the post–Cold War world the primary objective of arms control is to prevent the development by non-Western societies of military capabilities that could threaten Western interests. The West attempts to do this through international agreements, economic pressure and controls on the transfer of arms and weapons technologies.

The conflict between the West and the Confucian-Islamic states focuses largely, although not exclusively, on nuclear, chemical and biological weapons, ballistic missiles and other sophisticated means for delivering them, and the guidance, intelligence and other electronic capabilities for achieving that goal. The West promotes nonproliferation as a universal norm and nonproliferation treaties and inspections as means of realizing that norm. It also threatens a variety of sanctions against those who promote the spread of sophisticated weapons and proposes some benefits for those who do not. The attention of the West focuses, naturally, on nations that are actually or potentially hostile to the West.

The non-Western nations, on the other hand, assert their right to acquire and to deploy whatever weapons they think necessary for their security. They also have absorbed, to the full, the truth of the response of the Indian defense minister when asked what lesson he learned from the Gulf War: "Don't fight the United States unless you have nuclear weapons." Nuclear weapons, chemical weapons and missiles are viewed, probably erroneously, as the potential equalizer of superior Western conventional power. China, of course, already has nuclear weapons; Pakistan and India have the capability to deploy them. North Korea, Iran, Iraq, Libya and Algeria appear to be attempting to acquire them. A top Iranian official has declared that all Muslim states should acquire nuclear weapons, and in 1988 the president of Iran reportedly issued a directive calling for development of "offensive and defensive chemical, biological and radiological weapons."

Centrally important to the development of counter-West military capabilities is the sustained expansion of Chinas military power and its means to create military power. Buoyed by spectacular economic development, China is rapidly increasing its military spending and vigorously moving forward with the modernization of its armed forces. It is purchasing weapons from the former Soviet states; it is developing long-range missiles; in 1992 it tested a one-megaton nuclear device. It is developing power-projection capabilities, acquiring aerial refueling technology, and trying to purchase an aircraft carrier. Its military buildup and assertion of sovereignty over the South China Sea are provoking a multilateral regional arms race in East Asia. China is also a major exporter of arms and weapons technology. It has exported materials to Libya and Iraq that could be used to manufacture nuclear weapons and nerve gas. It has helped Algeria build a reactor suitable for nuclear weapons research and production. China has sold to Iran nuclear technology that American officials believe could only be used to create weapons and apparently has shipped components of 300-mile-range missiles to Pakistan. North Korea has had a nuclear weapons program under way for some while and has sold advanced missiles and missile technology to Syria and Iran. The flow of weapons and weapons technology is generally from East Asia to the Middle East. There is, however, some movement in the reverse direction; China has received Stinger missiles from Pakistan.

A Confucian-Islamic military connection has thus come into being, designed to promote acquisition by its members of the weapons and weapons technologies needed to counter the military power of the West. It may or may not last. At present, however, it is, as Dave McCurdy has said, "a renegades' mutual support pact, run by the proliferators and their backers." A new form of arms competition is thus occurring between Islamic-Confucian states and the West. In an old-fashioned arms race, each side developed its own arms to balance or to achieve superiority against the other side. In this new form of arms competition, one side is developing its arms and the other side is attempting not to balance but to limit and prevent that arms build-up while at the same time reducing its own military capabilities.

IMPLICATIONS FOR THE WEST

This article does not argue that civilization identities will replace all other identities, that nation states will disappear, that each civilization will become a single coherent political entity, that groups within a civilization will not conflict with and even fight each other. This paper does set forth the hypotheses that differences between civilizations are real and important; civilization-consciousness is increasing; conflict between civilizations will supplant ideological and other forms of conflict as the dominant global form of conflict; international relations, historically a game played out within Western civilization, will increasingly be de-Westernized and become a game in which non-Western civilizations are actors and not simply objects; successful political, security and economic international institutions are more likely to develop within civilizations than across civilizations; conflicts between groups in different civilizations will be more frequent, more sustained and more violent than conflicts between groups in the same civilization; violent conflicts between groups in different civilizations are the most likely and most dangerous source of escalation that could lead to global wars; the paramount axis of world politics will be the relations between "the West and the Rest"; the elites in some torn non-Western countries will try to make their countries part of the West, but in most cases face major obstacles to accomplishing this; a central focus of conflict for the immediate future will be between the West and several Islamic-Confucian states.

This is not to advocate the desirability of conflicts between civilizations. It is to set forth descriptive hypotheses as to what the future May be like. If these are plausible hypotheses, however, it is necessary to consider their implications for Western policy. These implications should be divided between short-term advantage and long-term accommodation. In the short term it is clearly in the interest of the West to promote greater cooperation and unity within its own civilization, particularly between its European and North American components; to incorporate into the West societies in Eastern Europe and Latin America whose cultures are close to those of the West; to promote and maintain cooperative relations with Russia and Japan; to prevent escalation of local inter-civilization conflicts into major inter-civilization wars; to limit the expansion of the military strength of Confucian and Islamic states; to moderate the reduction of Western military capabilities and maintain military superiority in East and Southwest Asia; to exploit differences and conflicts among Confucian and Islamic states; to support in other civilizations groups sympathetic to Western values and interests; to strengthen international institutions that reflect and legitimate Western interests and values and to promote the involvement of non-Western states in those institutions.

In the longer term other measures would be called for. Western civilization is both Western and modern. Non-Western civilizations have attempted to become modern without becoming Western. To date only Japan has fully succeeded in this quest. Non-Western civilizations will continue to attempt to acquire the wealth, technology, skills, machines and weapons that are part of being modern. They will also attempt to reconcile this modernity with their traditional culture and values. Their economic and military strength relative to the West will increase. Hence the West will increasingly have to accommodate these non-Western modern civilizations whose power approaches that of the West but whose values and interests differ significantly from those of the West. This will require the West to maintain the economic and military power necessary to protect its interests in relation to these civilizations. It will also, however, require the West to develop a more profound understanding of the basic religious and philosophical assumptions underlying other civilizations and the ways in which people in those civilizations see their interests. It will require an effort to identify elements of commonality between Western and other civilizations. For the relevant future, there will be no universal civilization, but instead a world of different civilizations, each of which will have to learn to coexist with the others.

The Summoning

"But They Said, We Will Not Hearken."

Jeremiah 6: 17

Fouad Ajami

SEPTEMBER/OCTOBER 1993

In Joseph Conrad's *Youth,* a novella published at the turn of the century, Marlowe, the narrator, remembers when he first encountered "the East":

> And then, before I could open my lips, the East spoke to me, but it was in a Western voice. A torrent of words was poured into the enigmatical, the fateful silence; outlandish, angry words mixed with words and even whole sentences of good English, less strange but even more surprising. The voice swore and cursed violently; it riddled the solemn peace of the bay by a volley of abuse. It began by calling me Pig, and from that went crescendo into unmentionable adjectives—in English.

The young Marlowe knew that even the most remote civilization had been made and remade by the West, and taught new ways.

Not so Samuel P. Huntington. In a curious essay, "The Clash of Civilizations," Huntington has found his civilizations whole and intact, watertight under an eternal sky. Buried alive, as it were, during the years of the Cold War, these civilizations (Islamic, Slavic-Orthodox, Western, Confucian, Japanese, Hindu, etc.) rose as soon as the stone was rolled off, dusted themselves off,

FOUAD AJAMI is Majid Khadduri Professor of Middle Eastern Studies at the School of Advanced International Studies, The Johns Hopkins University and proceeded to claim the loyalty of their adherents. For this student of history and culture, civilizations have always seemed messy creatures. Furrows run across whole civilizations, across individuals themselves—that was modernity's verdict. But Huntington looks past all that. The crooked and meandering alleyways of the world are straightened out. With a sharp pencil and a steady hand Huntington marks out where one civilization ends and the wilderness of "the other" begins.

More surprising still is Huntington's attitude toward states, and their place in his scheme of things. From one of the most influential and brilliant students of the state and its national interest there now comes an essay that misses the slyness of states, the unsentimental and cold-blooded nature of so much of what they do as they pick their way through chaos. Despite the obligatory passage that states will remain "the most powerful actors in world affairs," states are written off, their place given over to clashing civilizations. In Huntington's words, "The next world war, if there is one, will be a war between civilizations."

THE POWER OF MODERNITY

Huntington's meditation is occasioned by his concern about the state of the West, its power and the terms of its engagement with "the rest."[1] "He who gives, dominates," the great historian Fernand Braudel observed of the traffic of civilizations. In making itself over the centuries, the West helped make the others as well. We have come to the end of this trail, Huntington is sure. He is impressed by the "de-Westernization" of societies,

---

[1] The West itself is unexamined in Huntington's essay. No fissures run through it. No multiculturalists are heard from. It is orderly within its ramparts. What doubts Huntington has about the will within the walls, he has kept within himself. He has assumed that his call to unity will be answered, for outside flutter the banners of the Saracens and the Confucians.

their "indigenization" and apparent willingness to go their own way. In his view of things such phenomena as the "Hinduization" of India and Islamic fundamentalism are ascendant. To these detours into "tradition" Huntington has assigned great force and power.

But Huntington is wrong. He has underestimated the tenacity of modernity and secularism in places that acquired these ways against great odds, always perilously close to the abyss, the darkness never far. India will not become a Hindu state. The inheritance of Indian secularism will hold. The vast middle class will defend it, keep the order intact to maintain India's—and its own—place in the modern world of nations. There exists in that anarchic polity an instinctive dread of playing with fires that might consume it. Hindu chauvinism may coarsen the public life of the country, but the state and the middle class that sustains it know that a detour into religious fanaticism is a fling with ruin. A resourceful middle class partakes of global culture and norms. A century has passed since the Indian bourgeoisie, through its political vehicle the Indian National Congress, set out to claim for itself and India a place among nations. Out of that long struggle to overturn British rule and the parallel struggle against "communalism," the advocates of the national idea built a large and durable state. They will not cede all this for a political kingdom of Hindu purity.

We have been hearing from the traditionalists, but we should not exaggerate their power, for traditions are often most insistent and loud when they rupture, when people no longer really believe and when age-old customs lose their ability to keep men and women at home. The phenomenon we have dubbed as Islamic fundamentalism is less a sign of resurgence than of panic and bewilderment and guilt that the border with "the other" has been crossed. Those young urban poor, half-educated in the cities of the Arab world, and their Sorbonne-educated lay preachers, can they be evidence of a genuine return to tradition? They crash Europe's and America's gates in search of liberty and work, and they rail against the sins of the West. It is easy to understand Huntington's frustration with this kind of complexity, with the strange mixture of attraction and repulsion that the West breeds, and his need to simplify matters, to mark out the borders of civilizations.

Tradition-mongering is no proof, though, that these civilizations outside the West are intact, or that their thrashing about is an indication of their vitality, or that they present a conventional threat of arms. Even so thorough and far-reaching an attack against Western hegemony as Iran's theocratic revolution could yet fail to wean that society from the culture of the West. That country's cruel revolution was born of the realization of the "armed Imam" that his people were being seduced by America's ways. The gates had been thrown wide open in the 1970s, and the high walls Ayatollah Khomeini built around his polity were a response to that cultural seduction. Swamped, Iran was "rescued" by men claiming authenticity as their banner. One extreme led to another.

"We prayed for the rain of mercy and received floods," was the way Mehdi Bazargan, the decent modernist who was Khomeini's first prime minister, put it. But the millennium has been brought down to earth, and the dream of a pan-Islamic revolt in Iran's image has vanished into the wind. The terror and the shabbiness have caught up with the utopia. Sudan could emulate the Iranian "revolutionary example." But this will only mean the further pauperization and ruin of a desperate land. There is no rehabilitation of the Iranian example.

A battle rages in Algeria, a society of the Mediterranean, close to Europe—a wine-producing country for that matter—and in Egypt between the secular powers that be and an Islamic alternative. But we should not rush to print with obituaries of these states. In Algeria the nomenklatura of the National Liberation Front failed and triggered a revolt of the young, the underclass and the excluded. The revolt raised an Islamic banner. Caught between a regime they despised and a reign of virtue they feared, the professionals and the women and the modernists of the middle class threw their support to the forces of "order." They hailed the army's crackdown on the Islamicists; they allowed the interruption of a democratic process sure to bring the Islamicists to power; they accepted the "liberties" protected by the repression, the devil you know rather than the one you don't.

The Algerian themes repeat in the Egyptian case, although Egypt's dilemma over its Islamicist opposition is not as acute. The Islamicists continue to hound the state, but they cannot bring it down. There is no likelihood that the Egyptian state— now riddled with enough complacency and corruption to try the celebrated patience and good humor of the Egyptians— will go under. This is an old and skeptical country. It knows better than to trust its fate to enforcers of radical religious dogma. These are not deep and secure structures of order that the national middle classes have put in place. But they will not be blown away overnight.

Nor will Turkey lose its way, turn its back on Europe and chase after some imperial temptation in the scorched domains of Central Asia. Huntington sells that country's modernity and secularism short when he writes that the Turks—rejecting Mecca and rejected by Brussels—are likely to head to Tashkent in search of a Pan-Turkic role. There is no journey to that imperial past. Ataturk severed that link with fury, pointed his country westward, embraced the civilization of Europe and did it without qualms or second thoughts. It is on Frankfurt and Bonn—and Washington—not on Baku and Tashkent that the attention of the Turks is fixed. The inheritors of Ataturk's legacy are too shrewd to go chasing after imperial glory, gathering about them the scattered domains of the Turkish peoples. After their European possessions were lost, the Turks clung to Thrace and to all that this link to Europe represents.

Huntington would have nations battle for civilizational ties and fidelities when they would rather scramble for their market shares, learn how to compete in a merciless world economy, provide jobs, move out of poverty. For their part, the "management gurus" and those who believe that the interests have vanquished the passions in today's world tell us that men want Sony, not soil.[2] There is a good deal of truth in what they say, a terrible exhaustion with utopias, a reluctance to set out on expeditions of principle or belief. It is hard to think of Russia, ravaged as it is by inflation, taking up the grand cause of a "second Byzantium," the bearer of the orthodox-Slavic torch.

And where is the Confucian world Huntington speaks of? In the busy and booming lands of the Pacific Rim, so much of politics and ideology has been sublimated into finance that the nations of East Asia have turned into veritable workshops. The civilization of Cathay is dead; the Indonesian archipelago is deaf to the call of the religious radicals in Tehran as it tries to catch up with Malaysia and Singapore. A different wind blows in the lands of the Pacific. In that world economics, not politics, is in command. The world is far less antiseptic than Lee Kuan Yew, the sage of Singapore, would want it to be. A nemesis could lie in wait for all the prosperity that the 1980s brought to the Pacific. But the lands of the Pacific Rim—protected, to be sure, by an American security umbrella—are not ready for a great falling out among the nations. And were troubles to visit that world they would erupt within its boundaries, not across civilizational lines.

The things and ways that the West took to "the rest"—those whole sentences of good English that Marlowe heard a century ago—have become the ways of the world. The secular idea, the

---

[2]Kenichi Ohmae, "Global Consumers Want Sony, Not Soil," *New Perspectives Quarterly*, Fall 1991.

state system and the balance of power, pop culture jumping tariff walls and barriers, the state as an instrument of welfare, all these have been internalized in the remotest places. We have stirred up the very storms into which we now ride.

THE WEAKNESS OF TRADITION

Nations "cheat": they juggle identities and interests. Their ways meander. One would think that the traffic of arms from North Korea and China to Libya and Iran and Syria shows this—that states will consort with any civilization, however alien, as long as the price is right and the goods are ready. Huntington turns this routine act of selfishness into a sinister "Confucian-Islamic connection." There are better explanations: the commerce of renegades, plain piracy, an "underground economy" that picks up the slack left by the great arms suppliers (the United States, Russia, Britain and France).

Contrast the way Huntington sees things with Braudel's depiction of the traffic between Christendom and Islam across the Mediterranean in the sixteenth century—and this was in a religious age, after the fall of Constantinople to the Turks and of Granada to the Spanish: "Men passed to and fro, indifferent to frontiers, states and creeds. They were more aware of the necessities for shipping and trade, the hazards of war and piracy, the opportunities for complicity or betrayal provided by circumstances."[3]

Those kinds of "complicities" and ambiguities are missing in Huntington's analysis. Civilizations are crammed into the nooks and crannies—and checkpoints—of the Balkans. Huntington goes where only the brave would venture, into that belt of mixed populations stretching from the Adriatic to the Baltic.

---

[3]Ferdinand Braudel, *The Mediterranean and the Mediterranean World in the Age of Philip II*, Vol. II, New York: Harper & Row, 1976, p. 759.

Countless nationalisms make their home there, all aggrieved, all possessed of memories of a fabled past and equally ready for the demagogues vowing to straighten a messy map. In the thicket of these pan-movements he finds the line that marked "the eastern boundary of Western Christianity in the year 1500." The scramble for turf between Croatian nationalism and its Serbian counterpart, their "joint venture" in carving up Bosnia, are made into a fight of the inheritors of Rome, Byzantium and Islam.

But why should we fall for this kind of determinism? "An outsider who travels the highway between Zagreb and Belgrade is struck not by the decisive historical fault line which falls across the lush Slavonian plain but by the opposite. Serbs and Croats speak the same language, give or take a few hundred words, have shared the same village way of life for centuries."[4] The cruel genius of Slobodan Milosevic and Franjo Tudjman, men on horseback familiar in lands and situations of distress, was to make their bids for power into grand civilizational undertakings—the ramparts of the Enlightenment defended against Islam or, in Tudjman's case, against the heirs of the Slavic-Orthodox faith. Differences had to be magnified. Once Tito, an equal opportunity oppressor, had passed from the scene, the balancing act among the nationalities was bound to come apart. Serbia had had a measure of hegemony in the old system. But of the world that loomed over the horizon—privatization and economic reform—the Serbs were less confident. The citizens of Sarajevo and the Croats and the Slovenes had a head start on the rural Serbs. And so the Serbs hacked at the new order of things with desperate abandon.

Some Muslim volunteers came to Bosnia, driven by faith and zeal. Huntington sees in these few stragglers the sweeping

---

[4]Michael Ignatieff, "The Balkan Tragedy," *New York Review of Books*, May 13, 1993.

power of "civilizational rallying," proof of the hold of what he calls the "kin-country syndrome." This is delusion. No Muslim cavalry was ever going to ride to the rescue. The Iranians may have railed about holy warfare, but the Chetniks went on with their work. The work of order and mercy would have had to be done by the United States if the cruel utopia of the Serbs was to be contested.

It should have taken no powers of prophecy to foretell where the fight in the Balkans would end. The abandonment of Bosnia was of a piece with the ways of the world. No one wanted to die for Srebrenica. The Europeans averted their gaze, as has been their habit. The Americans hesitated for a moment as the urge to stay out of the Balkans did battle with the scenes of horror. Then "prudence" won out. Milosevic and Tudjman may need civilizational legends, but there is no need to invest their projects of conquest with this kind of meaning.

In his urge to find that relentless war across Islam's "bloody borders," Huntington buys Saddam Hussein's interpretation of the Gulf War. It was, for Saddam and Huntington, a civilizational battle. But the Gulf War's verdict was entirely different. For if there was a campaign that laid bare the interests of states, the lengths to which they will go to restore a tolerable balance of power in a place that matters, this was it. A local despot had risen close to the wealth of the Persian Gulf, and a Great Power from afar had come to the rescue. The posse assembled by the Americans had Saudi, Turkish, Egyptian, Syrian, French, British and other riders.

True enough, when Saddam Hussein's dream of hegemony was shattered, the avowed secularist who had devastated the ulama, the men of religion in his country, fell back on Ayatollah Khomeini's language of fire and brimstone and borrowed the symbolism and battle cry of his old Iranian nemesis. But few, if any, were fooled by this sudden conversion to the faith. They knew the predator for what he was: he had a Christian foreign minister (Tariq Aziz); he had warred against the Iranian revolution for nearly a decade and had prided himself on the secularism of his regime. Prudent men of the social and political order, the ulama got out of the way and gave their state the room it needed to check the predator at the Saudi/Kuwaiti border.[5] They knew this was one of those moments when purity bows to necessity. Ten days after Saddam swept into Kuwait, Saudi Arabia's most authoritative religious body, the Council of Higher Ulama, issued a *fatwa*, or a ruling opinion, supporting the presence of Arab and Islamic and "other friendly forces." All means of defense, the ulama ruled, were legitimate to guarantee the people "the safety of their religion, their wealth, and their honor and their blood, to protect what they enjoy of safety and stability." At some remove, in Egypt, that country's leading religious figure, the Shaykh of Al Ashar, Shaykh Jadd al Haqq, denounced Saddam as a tyrant and brushed aside his Islamic pretensions as a cover for tyranny.

Nor can the chief Iranian religious leader Ayatollah Ali Khamenei's rhetoric against the Americans during the Gulf War be taken as evidence of Iran's disposition toward that campaign. Crafty men, Iran's rulers sat out that war. They stood to emerge as the principal beneficiaries of Iraq's defeat. The American-led campaign against Iraq held out the promise of tilting the regional balance in their favor. No tears were shed in Iran for what befell Saddam Hussein's regime.

It is the mixed gift of living in hard places that men and women know how to distinguish between what they hear and what there is: no illusions were thus entertained in vast stretches of the Arab Muslim world about Saddam, or about

---

[5]Huntington quotes one Safar al Hawali, a religious radical at Umm al Qura University in Mecca, to the effect that the campaign against Iraq was another Western campaign against Islam. But this can't do as evidence. Safar al Hawali was a crank. Among the *ulama* class and the religious scholars in Saudi Arabia he was, for all practical purposes, a loner.

the campaign to thwart him for that matter. The fight in the gulf was seen for what it was: a bid for primacy met by an imperial expedition that laid it to waste. A circle was closed in the gulf: where once the order in the region "east of Suez" had been the work of the British, it was now provided by Pax Americana. The new power standing sentry in the gulf belonged to the civilization of the West, as did the prior one. But the American presence had the anxious consent of the Arab lands of the Persian Gulf. The stranger coming in to check the kinsmen.

The world of Islam divides and subdivides. The battle lines in the Caucasus, too, are not coextensive with civilizational fault lines. The lines follow the interests of states. Where Huntington sees a civilizational duel between Armenia and Azerbaijan, the Iranian state has cast religious zeal and fidelity to the wind. Indeed, in that battle the Iranians have tilted toward Christian Armenia.

THE WRIT OF STATES

We have been delivered into a new world, to be sure. But it is not a world where the writ of civilizations runs. Civilizations and civilizational fidelities remain. There is to them an astonishing measure of permanence. But let us be clear: civilizations do not control states, states control civilizations. States avert their gaze from blood ties when they need to; they see brotherhood and faith and kin when it is in their interest to do so.

We remain in a world of self-help. The solitude of states continues; the disorder in the contemporary world has rendered that solitude more pronounced. No way has yet been found to reconcile France to Pax Americana's hegemony, or to convince it to trust its security or cede its judgment to the preeminent Western power. And no Azeri has come up with a way the lands of Islam could be rallied to the fight over Nagorno Karabakh. The sky has not fallen in Kuala Lumpur or in Tunis over the setbacks of Azerbaijan in its fight with Armenia.

The lesson bequeathed us by Thucydides in his celebrated dialogue between the Melians and the Athenians remains. The Melians, it will be recalled, were a colony of the Lacedaemonians. Besieged by Athens, they held out and were sure that the Lacedaemonians were "bound, if only for very shame, to come to the aid of their kindred." The Melians never wavered in their confidence in their "civilizational" allies: "Our common blood insures our fidelity."[6] We know what became of the Melians. Their allies did not turn up, their island was sacked, their world laid to waste.

---

[6]Thucydides, *The Peloponnesian War*, New York: The Modern American Library, 1951, pp. 334–335.

The Dangers of Decadence

What the Rest Can Teach the West

Kishore Mahbubani

SEPTEMBER/OCTOBER 1993

In key Western capitals there is a deep sense of unease about the future. The confidence that the West would remain a dominant force in the 21st century, as it has for the past four or five centuries, is giving way to a sense of foreboding that forces like the emergence of fundamentalist Islam, the rise of East Asia and the collapse of Russia and Eastern Europe could pose real threats to the West. A siege mentality is developing. Within these troubled walls, Samuel P. Huntington's essay "The Clash of Civilizations?" is bound to resonate. It will therefore come as a great surprise to many Westerners to learn that the rest of the world fears the West even more than the West fears it, especially the threat posed by a wounded West.

Huntington is right: power is shifting among civilizations. But when the tectonic plates of world history move in a dramatic fashion, as they do now, perceptions of these changes depend on where one stands. The key purpose of this essay is to sensitize Western audiences to the perceptions of the rest of the world.

KISHORE MAHBUBANI, Deputy Secretary of Foreign Affairs and Dean of the Civil Service College, Singapore, last served overseas as Singapore's Permanent Representative to the United Nations (1984–89). These are his personal views.

The retreat of the West is not universally welcomed. There is still no substitute for Western leadership, especially American leadership. Sudden withdrawals of American support from Middle Eastern or Pacific allies, albeit unlikely, could trigger massive changes that no one would relish. Western retreat could be as damaging as Western domination.

By any historical standard, the recent epoch of Western domination, especially under American leadership, has been remarkably benign. One dreads to think what the world would have looked like if either Nazi Germany or Stalinist Russia had triumphed in what have been called the "Western civil wars" of the twentieth century. Paradoxically, the benign nature of Western domination may be the source of many problems. Today most Western policymakers, who are children of this era, cannot conceive of the possibility that their own words and deeds could lead to evil, not good. The Western media aggravate this genuine blindness. Most Western journalists travel overseas with Western assumptions. They cannot understand how the West could be seen as anything but benevolent. CNN is not the solution. The same visual images transmitted simultaneously into living rooms across the globe can trigger opposing perceptions. Western living rooms applaud when cruise missiles strike Baghdad. Most living outside see that the West will deliver swift retribution to nonwhite Iraqis or Somalis but not to white Serbians, a dangerous signal by any standard.

THE ASIAN HORDES

Huntington discusses the challenge posed by Islamic and Confucian civilizations. Since the bombing of the World Trade Center, Americans have begun to absorb European paranoia about Islam, perceived as a force of darkness hovering over a virtuous Christian civilization. It is ironic that the West should increasingly fear Islam when daily the Muslims are reminded of their own weakness. "Islam has bloody borders," Huntington says. But in all conflicts between Muslims and pro-Western forces, the Muslims are losing, and losing badly, whether they be Azeris, Palestinians, Iraqis, Iranians or Bosnian Muslims. With so much disunity, the Islamic world is not about to coalesce into a single force;

Oddly, for all this paranoia, the West seems to be almost deliberately pursuing a course designed to aggravate the Islamic world. The West protests the reversal of democracy in Myanmar, Peru or Nigeria, but not in Algeria. These double standards hurt. Bosnia has wreaked incalculable damage. The dramatic passivity of powerful European nations as genocide is committed on their doorstep has torn away the thin veil of moral authority that the West had spun around itself as a legacy of its recent benign era. Few can believe that the West would have remained equally passive if Muslim artillery shells had been raining down on Christian populations in Sarajevo or Srebrenica.

Western behavior toward China has been equally puzzling. In the 1970s, the West developed a love affair with a China ruled by a regime that had committed gross atrocities during the Great Leap Forward and the Cultural Revolution. But when Mao Zedong's disastrous rule was followed by a far more benign Deng Xiaoping era, the West punished China for what by its historical standards was a minor crackdown: the Tiananmen incident.

Unfortunately, Tiananmen has become a contemporary Western legend, created by live telecasts of the crackdown. Beijing erred badly in its excessive use of firearms but it did not err in its decision to crack down. Failure to quash the student rebellion could have led to political disintegration and chaos, a perennial Chinese nightmare. Western policymakers concede this in private. They are also aware of the dishonesty of some Western journalists: dining with student dissidents and even egging them on before reporting on their purported "hunger strike." No major Western journal has exposed such dishonesty or developed the political courage to say that China had virtually no choice in Tiananmen. Instead sanctions were imposed, threatening China's modernization. Asians see that Western public opinion—deified in Western democracy—can produce irrational consequences. They watch with trepidation as Western policies on China lurch to and fro, threatening the otherwise smooth progress of East Asia.

Few in the West are aware that the West is responsible for aggravating turbulence among the more than two billion people living in Islamic and Chinese civilizations. Instead, conjuring up images of the two Asian hordes that Western minds fear most—two forces that invaded Europe, the Muslims and the Mongols—Huntington posits a Confucian-Islamic connection against the West. American arms sales to Saudi Arabia do not suggest a natural Christian-Islamic connection. Neither should Chinese arms sales to Iran. Both are opportunistic moves, based not on natural empathy or civilizational alliances. The real tragedy of suggesting a Confucian-Islamic connection is that it obscures the fundamentally different nature of the challenge posed by these forces. The Islamic world will have great difficulty modernizing. Until then its turbulence will spill over into the West. East Asia, including China, is poised to achieve parity with the West. The simple truth is that East and Southeast Asia feel more comfortable with the West.

This failure to develop a viable strategy to deal with Islam or China reveals a fatal flaw in the West: an inability to come to terms with the shifts in the relative weights of civilizations that Huntington well documents. Two key sentences in Huntington's essay, when put side by side, illustrate the nature of the problem: first, "In the politics of civilizations, the peoples and governments of non-Western civilization no longer remain the objects of history as targets of Western colonization but join the

West as movers and shapers of history," and second, "The West in effect is using international institutions, military power and economic resources to run the world in ways that will maintain Western predominance, protect Western interests and promote Western political and economic values." This combination is a prescription for disaster.

Simple arithmetic demonstrates Western folly. The West has 800 million people; the rest make up almost 4.7 billion. In the national arena, no Western society would accept a situation where 15 percent of its population legislated for the remaining 85 percent. But this is what the West is trying to do globally.

Tragically, the West is turning its back on the Third World just when it can finally help the West out of its economic doldrums. The developing world's dollar output increased in 1992 more than that of North America, the European Community and Japan put together. Two-thirds of the increase in U.S. exports has gone to the developing world. Instead of encouraging this global momentum by completing the Uruguay Round, the West is doing the opposite. It is trying to create barriers, not remove them. French Prime Minister Edouard Balladur tried to justify this move by saying bluntly in Washington that the "question now is how to organize to protect ourselves from countries whose different values enable them to undercut us."

THE WEST'S OWN UNDOING

Huntington fails to ask one obvious question: If other civilizations have been around for centuries, why are they posing a challenge only now? A sincere attempt to answer this question reveals a fatal flaw that has recently developed in the Western mind: an inability to conceive that the West may have developed structural weaknesses in its core value systems and institutions. This flaw explains, in part, the recent rush to embrace the assumption that history has ended with the triumph of the Western ideal: individual freedom and democracy would always guarantee that Western civilization would stay ahead of the pack.

Only hubris can explain why so many Western societies are trying to defy the economic laws of gravity. Budgetary discipline is disappearing. Expensive social programs and pork-barrel projects multiply with little heed to costs. The West's low savings and investment rates lead to declining competitiveness vis-à-vis East Asia. The work ethic is eroding, while politicians delude workers into believing that they can retain high wages despite becoming internationally uncompetitive. Leadership is lacking. Any politician who states hard truths is immediately voted out. Americans freely admit that many of their economic problems arise from the inherent gridlock of American democracy. While the rest of the world is puzzled by these fiscal follies, American politicians and journalists travel around the world preaching the virtues of democracy. It makes for a curious sight.

The same hero-worship is given to the idea of individual freedom. Much good has come from this idea. Slavery ended. Universal franchise followed. But freedom does not only solve problems; it can also cause them. The United States has undertaken a massive social experiment, tearing down social institution after social institution that restrained the individual. The results have been disastrous. Since 1960 the U.S. population has increased 41 percent while violent crime has risen by 560 percent, single-mother births by 419 percent, divorce rates by 300 percent and the percentage of children living in single-parent homes by 300 percent. This is massive social decay. Many a society shudders at the prospects of this happening on its shores. But instead of traveling overseas with humility, Americans confidently preach the virtues of unfettered individual freedom, blithely ignoring the visible social consequences.

The West is still the repository of the greatest assets and

achievements of human civilization. Many Western values explain the spectacular advance of mankind: the belief in scientific inquiry, the search for rational solutions and the willingness to challenge assumptions. But a belief that a society is practicing these values can lead to a unique blindness: the inability to realize that some of the values that come with this package may be harmful. Western values do not form a seamless web. Some are good. Some are bad. But one has to stand outside the West to see this clearly, and to see how the West is bringing about its relative decline by its own hand. Huntington, too, is blind to this.

The Case for Optimism

The West Should Believe in Itself

Robert L. Bartley

SEPTEMBER/OCTOBER 1993

On November 9, 1989, our era ended. The breaching of the Berlin Wall sounded the end of not merely the Cold War, but an epoch of global conflict that started with the assassination of Archduke Francis Ferdinand on June 28, 1914. Now, with the twentieth century truncated, we are straining to discern the shape of the 21st.

We should remember that while there is of course always conflict and strife, not all centuries are as bloody as ours has been. The assassination in Sarajevo shattered an extraordinary period of economic, artistic and moral advance. It was a period when serious thinkers could imagine world economic unity bringing an end to wars. The conventional wisdom, as Keynes would later write, considered peace and prosperity "as normal, certain, and permanent, except in the direction of further improvement, and any deviation from [this course] as aberrant, scandalous, and avoidable."

If with benefit of hindsight this optimism seems wildly naïve, what will future generations make of the crabbed pessimism of today's conventional wisdom? Exhausted and jaded by our labors and trials, we now probe the dawning era for evidence

ROBERT L. BARTLEY is Editor of *The Wall Street Journal*.

not of relief but of new and even more ghastly horrors ahead. In particular, we have lost confidence in our own ability to shape the new era, and instead keep conjuring up inexorable historical and moral forces. Our public discourse is filled with guilt-ridden talk of global warming, the extinction of various species and Western decline.

Even so hardheaded a thinker as Samuel P. Huntington has concluded, "A West at the peak of its power confronts non-Wests that increasingly have the desire, the will and the resources to shape the world in non-Western ways." The conflicts of the future will be between "the West and the rest," the West and the Muslims, the West and an Islamic-Confucian alliance, or the West and a collection of other civilizations, including Hindu, Japanese, Latin American and Slavic-Orthodox.

This "clash of civilizations" does not sound like a pleasant 21st century. The conflicts will not be over resources, where it is always possible to split the difference, but over fundamental and often irreconcilable values. And in this competition the United States and the West will inevitably be on the defensive, since "the values that are most important in the West are the least important worldwide."

Well, perhaps. But is it really clear that the greatest potential for conflict lies between civilizations instead of within them? Despite the economic miracle of China's Guangdong province, are we really confident that the Confucians have mastered the trick of governing a billion people in one political entity? Do the women of Iran really long for the chador, or is it just possible the people of "the rest" will ultimately be attracted to the values of the West?

Undeniably there is an upsurge of interest in cultural, ethnic and religious values, notably but not solely in Islamic fundamentalism. But at the same time there are powerful forces toward world integration. Instant communications now span the globe. We watch in real time the drama of Tiananmen

Square and Sarajevo (if not yet Lhasa or Dushanbe). Financial markets on a 24-hour schedule link the world's economies.

Western, which is to say American, popular culture for better or worse spans the globe as well. The new Japanese crown princess was educated at Harvard, and the latest sumo sensation is known as Akebone, but played basketball as Chad Rowen. The world's language is English. Even the standard-bearers of "the rest"were largely educated in the West. Boatloads of immigrants, perhaps the true hallmark of the 21st century, land on the beaches of New York's Long Island.

This environment is not a happy one for governments of traditional nation states. In 1982 François Mitterrand found how markets limit national economic policy. A national currency—which is to say an independent monetary policy—is possible at sustainable cost only for the United States, and even then within limits, as the Carter administration found in 1979. In Western Europe and the Western hemisphere, the demands of national security have ebbed with the Cold War. Transnational companies and regional development leave the nation-state searching for a mission, as Kenichi Ohmae has detailed. Robert Reich asks what makes an "American" corporation. Walter Wriston writes of "The Twilight of Sovereignty."

These difficulties confront all governments, but they are doubly acute for authoritarians, who depend on isolation to dominate their people. Democracy, the quintessentially Western form of government, spread with amazing speed throughout Latin America and the former communist bloc and into Africa and Asia. In 1993 Freedom House reports 75 free nations, up from 55 a decade earlier, with only 31 percent of the world's population, and most of that in China, living under repressive regimes, down from 44 percent ten years ago. The combination of instant information, economic interdependence and the appeal of individual freedom is not a force to be taken lightly.

After all, it has just toppled the most powerful totalitarian empire history has known.

It is precisely the onslaught of this world civilization, of course, that provokes such reactions as Islamic fundamentalism. The mullahs profess to reject the decadent West, but their underlying quarrel is with modernity. Perhaps they have the "will and resources" to construct an alternative, and perhaps so does the geriatric regime in Beijing. But they face a deep dilemma indeed, for Western civilization and its political appendages of democracy and personal freedom are profoundly linked with the capitalist formula that is *the* formula for economic development.

THE POWER OF PROSPERITY

If you list the Freedom House rankings by per-capita annual income, you find that above figures equivalent to about $5,500, nearly all nations are democratic. The exceptions are the medieval oil sheikhdoms and a few Asian tigers such as Singapore. Even among the latter, development is leading to pressures for more freedom. Under Roh Tae Woo South Korea has deserted to full democracy. Nor should the implosion of the Liberal Democratic Party in Japan be comforting to advocates of some "consensual"model of democracy. Singapore's Lee Kuan Yew may be right to consider himself a philosopher king, but since Plato the species has been endangered and unreliable.

Perhaps Western values are an artifact of an exogenous civilization, but there is a powerful argument that they are an artifact of economic development itself. Development creates a middle class that wants a say in its own future, that cares about the progress and freedom of its sons and daughters. Since economic progress depends principally on this same group, with its drive for education and creative abilities, this desire can be suppressed only at the expense of development.

In the early stages of development, as for example in Guang-dong, the ruling elites may be able to forge an accommodation with the middle class, particularly if local military authorities are dealt into the action. But if the Chinese accommodation survives, it will be the first one. The attempt to incorporate the six million Hong Kong Chinese, with their increasingly evident expectation of self-rule, will be particularly disruptive. The lesson of other successfully developing nations is that continued progress depends on a gradual accommodation with democracy. And history teaches another profoundly optimistic lesson: as Huntington himself has been known to observe, democracies almost never go to war with each other.

The dominant flow of historical forces in the 21st century could well be this: economic development leads to demands for democracy and individual (or familial) autonomy; instant worldwide communications reduces the power of oppressive governments; the spread of democratic states diminishes the potential for conflict. The optimists of 1910, in other words, may turn out to have been merely premature.

STAYING THE COURSE

This future is of course no sure thing. Perhaps Huntington's forces of disintegration will in the end prevail, but that is no sure thing either. The West, above all the United States, and above even that the elites who read this journal, have the capacity to influence which of these futures is more likely. If the fears prevail, it will be in no small part because they lacked the will and wit to bring the hopes to reality.

The American foreign policy elite is in a sense the victim of its own success. Much to its own surprise, it won the Cold War. The classic containment policy outlined in George Kennan's "X" article and Paul Nitze's NSC-68 worked precisely as advertised, albeit after 40 years rather than the 10 to 15 Kennan predicted. But after its success, this compass is no longer relevant; as we enter the 21st century, our policy debate is adrift without a vision.

Some observations above hint at one such vision: if democracies do not fight each other, their spread not only fulfills our ideals but also promotes our security interests. The era of peace before 1914 was forged by the Royal Navy, the pound sterling and free trade. The essence of the task for the new era is to strike a balance between realpolitik and moralism.

Traditional diplomacy centers on relations among sovereign nation states, the internal character of which is irrelevant. In an information age, dominated by people-to-people contacts, policy should and will edge cautiously toward the moralistic, Wilsonian pole. Cautiously because as always this carries a risk of mindlessness. We cannot ignore military power; nothing could do more to give us freedom of action in the 21st century than a ballistic missile defense, whether or not you call it Star Wars. And while we need a human rights policy, applying it merely because we have access and leverage risks undermining, say, Egypt and Turkey, the bulwarks against an Islamic fundamentalism more detrimental to freedom and less susceptible to Western influence.

It will be a difficult balance to strike The case for optimism is admittedly not easy to sustain. Plumbing the temper of our elites and the state of debate, it is easier to give credence to Huntington's fears. But then, during the Hungarian revolution or Vietnam or the Pershing missile crisis, who would have thought that the West would stay the course it set out in NSC-68? It did, and to do so again it needs only to believe in itself.

Civilization Grafting

No Culture Is an Island

Liu Binyan

SEPTEMBER/OCTOBER 1993

The end of the Cold War has indeed brought about a new phase in world politics, yet its impact is not unidirectional. The tense confrontation between the two armed camps has disappeared and in this sense ideological conflict seems to have come to an end, for the moment. But conflicts of economic and political interests are becoming more and more common among the major nations of the world, and more and more tense. Neither civilization nor culture has become the "fundamental source of conflict in this new world."

The new world is beginning to resemble the one in which I grew up in the 1930s. Of course, tremendous changes have taken place; nonetheless there are increasing similarities. Western capitalism has changed greatly, but the current global recession is in many ways similar to the Great Depression. The Soviet Union and Nazi Germany may no longer exist, but the economic, social and political factors that led to their emergence still do—economic dislocation, xenophobia and populism.

The Cold War has ended, but hot wars rage in more than thirty countries and regions. The wave of immigrants from

LIU BINYAN, one of China's leading dissidents, is Director of the Princeton China Initiative, Princeton, New Jersey. His most recent book is *A Higher Kind of Loyalty: A Memoir*.

poor territories to rich countries and the influx of people from rural areas to cities have reached an unprecedented scale, forming what the UN Population Fund has called the "current crisis of mankind." We can hardly say these phenomena result from conflict between different civilizations.

CHINA'S ERRANT EXPERIMENT

For most countries the task is not to demarcate civilizations but to mix and meld them. In the former colonial countries, the problems of poverty and starvation have never been solved by their own civilizations or by the interaction of their indigenous civilization with Western civilization. But this search for a successful formula for economic well-being and political freedom continues.

Look at China. The Chinese people eagerly embraced Communism in the pursuit of economic development and political dignity. The bankruptcy of Maoism and socialism occurred a dozen years before the collapse of the former Soviet Union. It was not the result of the end of the Cold War, but the disaster brought about by Maoist ideology. The reason for this shift again comes from the strong desire of the people to get rid of poverty and to gain freedom. For China this is the third time people have tried to graft Western civilization onto traditional civilization—in the first half of the twentieth century and in the 1980s, with capitalism; from the late 1940s to the 1970s, with Marxism-Leninism.

Now, though Confucianism is gradually coming back to China, it cannot be compared to the increasingly forceful influence of Western culture on the Chinese people in the last twenty years. The Chinese people are a practical sort; they have always been concerned about their material well-being. In addition, the last forty years have left them wary of intangible philosophies, gods and ideals. Nowhere in China is there a group or political faction that could be likened to the extreme nationalists of Russia or Europe.

Nor can we expect any civilizational unity that will bring the Confucian world together. In the past forty years, the split of mainland China with Taiwan was of course due to political and ideological differences. After the end of the Cold War the Confucianist culture common to the Chinese from both sides of the Taiwan Strait will not overcome the differences in political systems, ideology and economic development.

Deng Xiaoping's experiment is to try to weld Western capitalism with Marxism-Leninism and even aspects of Confucianism. Thus while liberalizing the economy, the Chinese communist regime also points to the consumerism and hedonism of Western civilization in an effort to resist the influences of democracy and freedom. At the same time, it borrows from Confucianist thought—obedience to superiors, etc.—which is useful in stabilizing communist rule. It also attempts to use Chinese nationalist sentiments in place of a bankrupt ideology, seeking to postpone its inevitable collapse.

There are many historical and current examples of rulers who have a greater interest in maintaining or developing some kind of traditional order rather than in accommodating the struggles and changing interests of ordinary people. In the mid-1930s, Chang Kai-shek launched a national campaign advocating Confucianism—called "The Movement of New Life"—when China's population was victimized by famine, civil war and Japanese aggression. The movement aimed to distract people from their real interests and ended in complete failure. Since the 1980s China's new rulers began a campaign similar to the KMT's—"The Movement for Higher Spiritual Civilization"— which advocated love for the country and the party, and behaving civilly toward others. But the actual aim of the campaign was to replace the bankrupt ideology and to distract the public from its interest in democracy and freedom, and to blunt the cultural and moral impact of the West. Understandably, it failed. Even the terminology of a "spiritual civilization" became the target of irony and ridicule among the Chinese.

What will emerge in China is a mixture of these many forces, but it will not be the kind of mixture that this regime wants. It will not mix economic freedom with political unfreedom. Communism and capitalism are so completely different that no one will be fooled for long that they can be joined. In the end there will be a Chinese path, but it will be a different path to freedom, a different path to democracy. The Chinese people do not speak in Western phrases and political philosophies, but they know what kind of political and economic system best serves their own welfare.

TAKING THE BEST FROM EACH

It is ironic that Samuel P. Huntington sees a resurgent Confucianism at the very time when spiritual deterioration and moral degradation are eroding China's cultural foundation. Forty-seven years of communist rule have destroyed religion, education, the rule of law, and morality. Today this dehumanization caused by the despotism, absolute poverty and asceticism of the Mao era is evidenced in the rampant lust for power, money and carnal pleasures among many Chinese.

Coping with this moral and spiritual vacuum is a problem not just for China but for all civilizations. Will the 21st century be an era when, through interaction and consensus, civilizations can merge, thus helping peoples to break old cycles of dehumanization? Getting rid of poverty and slavery is the least of China's problems. The more difficult task is the process of men's self-salvation, that is, transforming underlings and cowed peoples into human beings. Enriching the human spirit is indeed the longer and harder task. It will require using the best of all civilizations, not emphasizing the differences between them.

The Modernizing Imperative

Tradition and Change

Jeane J. Kirkpatrick

SEPTEMBER/OCTOBER 1993

I approach the work of Samuel P. Huntington with keen interest and high expectations. Like most political scientists, I have learned much from his writings. Now in his article "The Clash of Civilizations?" he once again raises new questions.

In his essay, Huntington asserts that civilizations are real and important and predicts that "conflict between civilizations will supplant ideological and other forms of conflict as the dominant global form of conflict." He further argues that institutions for cooperation will be more likely to develop within civilizations, and conflicts will most often arise between groups in different civilizations. These strike me as interesting but dubious propositions.

Huntington's classification of contemporary civilizations is questionable. He identifies "seven or eight major civilizations" in the contemporary world: Western (which includes both European and North American variants), Confucian, Japanese, Islamic, Hindu, Slavic-Orthodox, Latin American "and

JEANE J. KIRKPATRICK is Leavey Professor of Government at Georgetown University and Senior Fellow at the American Enterprise Institute.

possibly African."

This is a strange list.

If civilization is defined by common objective elements such as language, history, religion, customs and institutions and, subjectively, by identification, and if it is the broadest collectivity with which persons intensely identify, why distinguish "Latin American" from "Western"civilization? Like North America, Latin America is a continent settled by Europeans who brought with them European languages and a European version of Judeo-Christian religion, law, literature and gender roles. The Indian component in Latin American culture is more important in some countries (Mexico, Guatemala, Ecuador and Peru) than in North America. But the African influence is more important in the United States than in all but a few Latin American countries (Brazil, Belize and Cuba). Both North and South America are "Western" European with an admixture of other elements.

And what is Russia if not "Western"? The East/West designations of the Cold War made sense in a European context, but in a global context Slavic/Orthodox people are Europeans who share in Western culture. Orthodox theology and liturgy, Leninism and Tolstoy are expressions of Western culture.

It is also not clear that over the centuries differences between civilizations have led to the longest and most violent conflicts. At least in the twentieth century, the most violent conflicts have occurred within civilizations: Stalin's purges, Pol Pot's genocide, the Nazi holocaust and World War II. It could be argued that the war between the United States and Japan involved a clash of civilizations, but those differences had little role in that war. The Allied and Axis sides included both Asian and European members.

The liberation of Kuwait was no more a clash between civilizations than World War II or the Korean or Vietnamese wars. Like Korea and Vietnam, the Persian Gulf War pitted one non-Western Muslim government against another. Once aggression had occurred, the United States and other Western governments became involved for geopolitical reasons that transcended cultural differences. Saddam Hussein would like the world to believe otherwise.

After the United States mobilized an international coalition against Iraq, Saddam Hussein, until then the leader of a revolutionary secular regime, took to public prayers and appeals for solidarity to the Muslim world. Certain militant, anti-Western Islamic fundamentalists, Huntington reminds us, responded with assertions that it was a war of "the West against Islam." But few believed it. More governments of predominantly Muslim societies rallied to support Kuwait than to "save" Iraq.

In Bosnia, the efforts of Radovan Karadzic and other Serbian extremists to paint themselves as bulwarks against Islam are no more persuasive, although the passivity of the European Community, the United States, NATO and the United Nations in the face of Serbia's brutal aggression against Bosnia has finally stimulated some tangible Islamic solidarity. But most governments of predominantly Muslim states have been reluctant to treat the Bosnian conflict as a religious war. The Bosnian government itself has resisted any temptation to present its problem as Islam versus the Judeo-Christian world. The fact that Serbian forces began their offensive against Croatia and Slovenia should settle the question of Serbian motives and goals, which are territorial aggrandizement, not holy war.

Indubitably, important social, cultural and political differences exist between Muslim and Judeo-Christian civilizations. But the most important and explosive differences involving Muslims are found within the Muslim world—between persons, parties and governments who are reasonably moderate, nonexpansionist and nonviolent and those who are anti-modern and anti-Western, extremely intolerant, expansionist and violent. The first target of Islamic fundamentalists is not another civilization, but their own governments. "Please do not call them Muslim fundamentalists,"a deeply religious Muslim friend said to me. "They do not represent a more fundamental version of the Muslim religion. They are simply Muslims who are also violent political extremists."

Elsewhere as well, the conflict between fanaticism and constitutionalism, between totalitarian ambition and the rule of law, exists within civilizations in a clearer, purer form than between them. In Asia the most intense conflict may turn out to be between different versions of being Chinese or Indian.

Without a doubt, civilizations are important. By eroding the strength of local and national cultures and identifications, modernization enhances the importance of larger units of identification such as civilizations. Huntington is also surely right that global communication and stepped-up migration exacerbate conflict by bringing diametrically opposed values and life-styles into direct contact with one another. Immigration brings exotic practices into schools, neighborhoods and other institutions of daily life and challenges the cosmopolitanism of Western societies. Religious tolerance in the abstract is one thing; veiled girls in French schoolrooms are quite another. Such challenges are not welcome anywhere.

But Huntington, who has contributed so much to our understanding of modernization and political change, also knows the ways that modernization changes people, societies and politics. He knows the many ways that modernization equals Westernization—broadly conceived—and that it can produce backlash and bitter hostility. But he also knows how powerful is the momentum of modern, Western ways of science, technology, democracy and free markets. He knows that the great question for non-Western societies is whether they can be modern without being Western. He believes Japan has succeeded. Maybe.

He is probably right that most societies will simultaneously seek the benefits of modernization and of traditional relations. To the extent that they and we are successful in preserving our

traditions while accepting the endless changes of modernization, our differences from one another will be preserved, and
the need for not just a pluralistic society but a pluralistic world
will grow ever more acute.

Do Civilizations Hold?

Albert L. Weeks

SEPTEMBER/OCTOBER 1993

Samuel P. Huntington has resurrected an old controversy in the study of international affairs: the relationship between "microcosmic" and "macrocosmic" processes. Partisans of the former single out the nation state as the basic unit, or determining factor, in the yin and yang of world politics. The "macros," on the other hand, view world affairs on the lofty level of the civilizations to which nation states belong and by which their behavior is allegedly largely determined.

To one degree or another, much of the latter school's thinking, although they may be loath to admit it, derives from Oswald Spengler, Arnold Toynbee, Quincy Wright, F. N. Parkinson and others. In contrast, scholars such as Hans J. Morgenthau, John H. Herz and Raymond Aron have tended to hew to the "micro" school.

Both schools began debating the issue vigorously back in the 1950s. That Huntington is resurrecting the controversy 40 years later is symptomatic of the failure of globalism—specifically the idea of establishing a "new world order"—to take root and of the failure to make sense of contradictory trends and events. His aim is to find new, easily classified determinants of contemporary quasi-chaotic international behavior and thus to get a handle on the international kaleidoscope.

ALBERT L. WEEKS is Professor Emeritus of International Relations at New York University.

His methodology is not new. In arguing the macro case in the 1940s, Toynbee distinguished what he called primary, secondary and tertiary civilizations by the time of their appearance in history, contending that their attributes continued to influence contemporary events. Wright, likewise applying a historical method, classified civilizations as "bellicose" (including Syrian, Japanese and Mexican), "moderately bellicose" (Germanic, Western, Russian, Scandinavian, etc.) and "most peaceful" (such as Irish, Indian and Chinese). Like Toynbee and now Huntington, he attributed contemporary significance to these factors. Huntington's classification, while different in several respects from those of his illustrious predecessors, also identifies determinants on a grand scale by "civilizations."

His endeavor, however, has its own fault lines. The lines are the borders encompassing each distinct nation state and mercilessly chopping the alleged civilizations into pieces. With the cultural and religious glue of these "civilizations" thin and cracked, with the nation state's political regime providing the principal bonds, crisscross fracturing and cancellation of Huntington's own macro-scale, somewhat anachronistic fault lines are inevitable.

The world remains fractured along political and possibly geopolitical lines; cultural and historical determinants are a great deal less vital and virulent. Politics, regimes and ideologies are culturally, historically and "civilizationally" determined to an extent. But it is willful, day-to-day, crisis-to-crisis, war-to-war political decision-making by nation-state units that remains the single most identifiable determinant of events in the international arena. How else can we explain repeated nation-state "defections" from their collective "civilizations"? As Huntington himself points out, in the Persian Gulf War "one Arab state invaded another and then fought a coalition of Arab, Western and other states."

Raymond Aron described at length the primacy of a nation

state's political integrity and independence, its inviolable territoriality and sovereign impermeability. He observed that "men have believed that the fate of cultures was at stake on the battlefields at the same time as the fate of provinces." But, he added, the fact remains that sovereign states "are engaged in a competition for power [and] conquests . . . . In our times the major phenomenon [on the international scene] is the heterogeneity of state units [not] supranational aggregations."

The West Is Best

Gerard Piel

SEPTEMBER/OCTOBER 1993

We must be in terror of the civilizations conjured by Samuel P. Huntington for the same reason that Nils Bohr admonished us to fear ghosts: We see them, and we know they are not there!

We have another reason to be in terror of them. Without boundaries, interiors or exteriors, continuity or coherent entity, any of the Huntington civilizations can be summoned in a moment to ratify whatever action the West and its remaining superpower deem rightful. Now they fit the Eric Ericsson definition of the pseudo-species, outside the law.

In the end, "the West and the Rest" offers a more useful analysis. We can recognize these ghostly civilizations as the developing countries and the countries in transition.

They all aspire to the Western model. They are still engaged in conquest of the material world. As they proceed with their industrialization, they progressively embrace the "Western ideas," in Huntington's litany, "of individualism, liberalism, constitutionalism, human rights, equality, liberty, the rule of law, democracy, free markets . . . ."

At the primary level it is a function of lengthening life expectancy; people in those countries are beginning to live long enough to discover they have rights and to assert them. Mass education, which comes with Westernizing industrialization,

GERARD PIEL is Chairman Emeritus of Scientific American, Inc.

makes its contribution as well. Tiananmen Square in Beijing and the massing of the people at the parliament building in Moscow stand as rites in a passage.

How long the process will take depends on how the West responds to the needs and the disorder that beset the emerging and developing nations—in fear or in rational quest of the common future. The question is: Do Western ideas have more substance than those pseudo-civilizations?

Response

If Not Civilizations, What?

Paradigms of the Post-Cold War World

Samuel P. Huntington

NOVEMBER/DECEMBER 1993

When people think seriously, they think abstractly; they conjure up simplified pictures of reality called concepts, theories, models, paradigms. Without such intellectual constructs, there is, William James said, only "a bloomin' buzzin' confusion." Intellectual and scientific advance, as Thomas Kuhn showed in his classic *The Structure of Scientific Revolutions*, consists of the displacement of one paradigm, which has become increasingly incapable of explaining new or newly discovered facts, by a new paradigm that accounts for those facts in a more satisfactory fashion. "To be accepted as a paradigm," Kuhn wrote, "a theory must seem better than its competitors, but it need not,

SAMUEL P. HUNTINGTON is the Eaton Professor of the Science of Government and Director of the John M. Olin Institute for Strategic Studies at Harvard University. His article "The Clash of Civilizations?" appeared in the Summer 1993 issue of *Foreign Affairs*, and several responses to it were published in the September/October 1993 issue.

and in fact never does, explain all the facts with which it can be confronted."

For 40 years students and practitioners of international relations thought and acted in terms of a highly simplified but very useful picture of world affairs, the Cold War paradigm. The world was divided between one group of relatively wealthy and mostly democratic societies, led by the United States, engaged in a pervasive ideological, political, economic, and, at times, military conflict with another group of somewhat poorer, communist societies led by the Soviet Union. Much of this conflict occurred in the Third World outside of these two camps, composed of countries which often were poor, lacked political stability, were recently independent and claimed to be nonaligned. The Cold War paradigm could not account for everything that went on in world politics. There were many anomalies, to use Kuhn's term, and at times the paradigm blinded scholars and statesmen to major developments, such as the Sino-Soviet split. Yet as a simple model of global politics, it accounted for more important phenomena than any of its rivals; it was an indispensable starting point for thinking about international affairs; it came to be almost universally accepted; and it shaped thinking about world politics for two generations.

The dramatic events of the past five years have made that paradigm intellectual history. There is clearly a need for a new model that will help us to order and to understand central developments in world politics. What is the best simple map of the post-Cold War world?

A MAP OF THE NEW WORLD

"The Clash of Civilizations?" is an effort to lay out elements of a post-Cold War paradigm. As with any paradigm, there is much the civilization paradigm does not account for, and critics will have no trouble citing events—even important events like Iraq's invasion of Kuwait—that it does not explain and would not have predicted (although it would have predicted the evaporation of the anti-Iraq coalition after March 1991). Yet, as Kuhn demonstrates, anomalous events do not falsify a paradigm. A paradigm is disproved only by the creation of an alternative paradigm that accounts for more crucial facts in equally simple or simpler terms (that is, at a comparable level of intellectual abstraction; a more complex theory can always account for more things than a more parsimonious theory). The debates the civilizational paradigm has generated around the world show that, in some measure, it strikes home; it either accords with reality as people see it or it comes close enough so that people who do not accept it have to attack it.

What groupings of countries will be most important in world affairs and most relevant to understanding and making sense of global politics? Countries no longer belong to the Free World, the communist bloc, or the Third World. Simple two-way divisions of countries into rich and poor or democratic and nondemocratic may help some but not all that much. Global politics are now too complex to be stuffed into two pigeonholes. For reasons outlined in the original article, civilizations are the natural successors to the three worlds of the Cold War. At the macro level world politics are likely to involve conflicts and shifting power balances of states from different civilizations, and at the micro level the most violent, prolonged and dangerous (because of the possibility of escalation) conflicts are likely to be between states and groups from different civilizations. As the article pointed out, this civilization paradigm accounts for many important developments in international affairs in recent years, including the breakup of the Soviet Union and Yugoslavia, the wars going on in their former territories, the rise of religious fundamentalism throughout the world, the struggles within Russia, Turkey and Mexico over their identity, the intensity of the trade conflicts between the United States and Japan, the resistance of Islamic states to Western pressure on Iraq and Libya, the efforts of Islamic and Confucian states to acquire nuclear weapons and the means to deliver them, China's continuing role as an "outsider" great power, the consolidation of new democratic regimes in some countries and not in others, and the escalating arms race in East Asia.

In the few months since the article was written, the following events have occurred that also fit the civilizational paradigm and might have been predicted from it:

—the continuation and intensification of the fighting among Croats, Muslims and Serbs in the former Yugoslavia;

—the failure of the West to provide meaningful support to the Bosnian Muslims or to denounce Croat atrocities in the same way Serb atrocities were denounced;

—Russia's unwillingness to join other UN Security Council members in getting the Serbs in Croatia to make peace with the Croatian government, and the offer of Iran and other Muslim nations to provide 18,000 troops to protect Bosnian Muslims;

—the intensification of the war between Armenians and Azeris, Turkish and Iranian demands that the Armenians surrender their conquests, the deployment of Turkish troops to and Iranian troops across the Azerbaijan border, and Russia's warning that the Iranian action contributes to "escalation of the conflict" and "pushes it to dangerous limits of internationalization";

—the continued fighting in central Asia between Russian troops and Mujaheddin guerrillas;

—the confrontation at the Vienna Human Rights Conference between the West, led by U.S. Secretary of State Warren Christopher, denouncing "cultural relativism," and a coalition of Islamic and Confucian states rejecting "Western universalism";

—the refocusing in parallel fashion of Russian and NATO military planners on "the threat from the South";

—the voting, apparently almost entirely along civilizational lines, that gave the 2000 Olympics to Sydney rather than Beijing;

—the sale of missile components from China to Pakistan, the resulting imposition of U.S. sanctions against China, and the confrontation between China and the United States over the alleged shipment of nuclear technology to Iran;

—China's breaking the moratorium and testing a nuclear weapon, despite vigorous U.S. protests, and North Korea's refusal to participate further in talks on its own nuclear weapons program;

—the revelation that the U.S. State Department was following a "dual containment" policy directed at both Iran and Iraq;

—the announcement by the U.S. Defense Department of a new strategy of preparing for two "major regional conflicts," one against North Korea, the other against Iran or Iraq;

—the call by Iran's president for alliances with China and India so that "we can have the last word on international events";

—new German legislation drastically curtailing the admission of refugees;

—the agreement between Russian President Boris Yeltsin and Ukrainian President Leonid Kravchuk on the disposition of the Black Sea fleet and other issues;

—U.S. bombing of Baghdad, its virtually unanimous support by Western governments, and its condemnation by almost all Muslim governments as another example of the West's "double standard";

—the United States listing Sudan as a terrorist state and the indictment of Sheik Omar Abdel Rahman and his followers for conspiring "to levy a war of urban terrorism against the United States";

—the improved prospects for the eventual admission of Poland, Hungary, the Czech Republic and Slovakia into NATO.

Samuel P. Huntington

Does a "clash of civilizations" perspective account for everything of significance in world affairs during these past few months? Of course not. It could be argued, for instance, that the agreement between the Palestine Liberation Organization and the Israeli government on the Gaza Strip and Jericho is a dramatic anomaly to the civilizational paradigm, and in some sense it is. Such an event, however, does not invalidate a civilizational approach: it is historically significant precisely because it is between groups from two different civilizations who have been fighting each other for over four decades. Truces and limited agreements are as much a part of the clashes between civilizations as Soviet-American arms control agreements were part of the Cold War; and while the conflict between Jew and Arab may be circumscribed, it still continues.

Inter-civilizational issues are increasingly replacing inter-superpower issues as the top items on the international agenda. These issues include arms proliferation (particularly of weapons of mass destruction and the means of delivering them), human rights, and immigration. On these three issues, the West is on one side and most of the other major civilizations are on the other. President Clinton at the United Nations urges intensified efforts to curb nuclear and other unconventional weapons; Islamic and Confucian states plunge ahead in their efforts to acquire them; Russia practices ambivalence. The extent to which countries observe human rights corresponds overwhelmingly with divisions among civilizations: the West and Japan are highly protective of human rights; Latin America, India, Russia, and parts of Africa protect some human rights; China, many other Asian countries, and most Muslim societies are least protective of human rights. Rising immigration from non-Western sources is provoking rising concern in both Europe and America. Other European countries in addition to Germany are tightening their restrictions at the same time that the barriers to movement of people within the European

Community are rapidly disappearing. In the United States, massive waves of new immigrants are generating support for new controls, despite the fact that most studies show immigrants to be making a net positive contribution to the American economy.

AMERICA UNDONE?

One function of a paradigm is to highlight what is important (e.g., the potential for escalation in clashes between groups from different civilizations); another is to place familiar phenomena in a new perspective. In this respect, the civilizational paradigm may have implications for the United States.[1] Countries like the Soviet Union and Yugoslavia that bestride civilizational fault lines tend to come apart. The unity of the United States has historically rested on the twin bedrocks of European culture and political democracy. These have been essentials of America to which generations of immigrants have assimilated. The essence of the American creed has been equal rights for the individual, and historically immigrant and outcast groups have invoked and thereby reinvigorated the principles of the creed in their struggles for equal treatment in American society. The most notable and successful effort was the civil rights movement led by Martin Luther King, Jr., in the 1950s and 1960s. Subsequently, however, the demand shifted from equal rights for individuals to special rights (affirmative action and similar measures) for blacks and other groups. Such claims run directly counter to the underlying principles that have been the basis of American political unity; they reject the idea of a "color-blind" society of equal individuals and instead promote a "color-conscious" society with government-sanctioned privileges for some groups. In a parallel movement, intellectuals and

---

[1]See, for instance, the map in *Die Welt*, June 16, 1993, p. 3.

politicians began to push the ideology of "multiculturalism," and to insist on the rewriting of American political, social, and literary history from the viewpoint of non-European groups. At the extreme, this movement tends to elevate obscure leaders of minority groups to a level of importance equal to that of the Founding Fathers. Both the demands for special group rights and for multiculturalism encourage a clash of civilizations within the United States and encourage what Arthur M. Schlesinger, Jr., terms "the disuniting of America."

The United States is becoming increasingly diverse ethnically and racially. The Census Bureau estimates that by 2050 the American population will be 23 percent Hispanic, 16 percent black and 10 percent Asian-American. In the past the United States has successfully absorbed millions of immigrants from scores of countries because they adapted to the prevailing European culture and enthusiastically embraced the American Creed of liberty, equality, individualism, democracy. Will this pattern continue to prevail as 50 percent of the population becomes Hispanic or nonwhite? Will the new immigrants be assimilated into the hitherto dominant European culture of the United States? If they are not, if the United States becomes truly multicultural and pervaded with an internal clash of civilizations, will it survive as a liberal democracy? The political identity of the United States is rooted in the principles articulated in its founding documents. Will the de-Westernization of the United States, if it occurs, also mean its de-Americanization? If it does and Americans cease to adhere to their liberal democratic and European-rooted political ideology, the United States as we have known it will cease to exist and will follow the other ideologically defined superpower onto the ash heap of history.[2]

---

[2]For a brilliant and eloquent statement of why the future of the United States could be problematic, see Bruce D. Porter, "Can American Democracy Survive?," *Commentary*, November 1993, pp. 37-40.

If Not Civilizations, What?

GOT A BETTER IDEA?

A civilizational approach explains much and orders much of the "bloomin' buzzin' confusion" of the post-Cold War world, which is why it has attracted so much attention and generated so much debate around the world. Can any other paradigm do better? If not civilizations, what? The responses in *Foreign Affairs* to my article did not provide any compelling alternative picture of the world. At best they suggested one pseudo-alternative and one unreal alternative.

The pseudo-alternative is a statist paradigm that constructs a totally irrelevant and artificial opposition between states and civilizations: "Civilizations do not control states," says Fouad Ajami, "states control civilizations." But it is meaningless to talk about states and civilizations in terms of "control." States, of course, try to balance power, but if that is all they did, West European countries would have coalesced with the Soviet Union against the United States in the late 1940s. States respond primarily to perceived threats, and the West European states then saw a political and ideological threat from the East. As my original article argued, civilizations are composed of one or more states, and "Nation states will remain the most powerful actors in world affairs." Just as nation states generally belonged to one of three worlds in the Cold War, they also belong to civilizations. With the demise of the three worlds, nation states increasingly define their identity and their interests in civilizational terms, and West European peoples and states now see a cultural threat from the South replacing the ideological threat from the East.

We do not live in a world of countries characterized by the "solitude of states" (to use Ajami's phrase) with no connections between them. Our world is one of overlapping groupings of states brought together in varying degrees by history, culture, religion, language, location and institutions. At the broadest level these groupings are civilizations. To deny their existence is to deny the basic realities of human existence.

The unreal alternative is the one-world paradigm that a universal civilization now exists or is likely to exist in the coming years. Obviously people now have and for millennia have had common characteristics that distinguish humans from other species. These characteristics have always been compatible with the existence of very different cultures. The argument that a universal culture or civilization is now emerging takes various forms, none of which withstands even passing scrutiny.

First, there is the argument that the collapse of Soviet communism means the end of history and the universal victory of liberal democracy throughout the world. This argument suffers from the Single Alternative Fallacy. It is rooted in the Cold War assumption that the only alternative to communism is liberal democracy and that the demise of the first produces the universality of the second. Obviously, however, there are many forms of authoritarianism, nationalism, corporatism and market communism (as in China) that are alive and well in today's world. More significantly, there are all the religious alternatives that lie outside the world that is perceived in terms of secular ideologies. In the modern world, religion is a central, perhaps *the* central, force that motivates and mobilizes people. It is sheer hubris to think that because Soviet communism has collapsed the West has won the world for all time.

Second, there is the assumption that increased interaction—greater communication and transportation—produces a common culture. In some circumstances this may be the case. But wars occur most frequently between societies with high levels of interaction, and interaction frequently reinforces existing identities and produces resistance, reaction and confrontation.

Third, there is the assumption that modernization and economic development have a homogenizing effect and produce a common modern culture closely resembling that which has existed in the West in this century. Clearly, modern urban, literate, wealthy, industrialized societies do share cultural traits that distinguish them from backward, rural, poor, undeveloped societies. In the contemporary world most modern societies have been Western societies. But modernization does not equal Westernization. Japan, Singapore and Saudi Arabia are modern, prosperous societies but they clearly are non-Western. The presumption of Westerners that other peoples who modernize must become "like us" is a bit of Western arrogance that in itself illustrates the clash of civilizations. To argue that Slovenes and Serbs, Arabs and Jews, Hindus and Muslims, Russians and Tajiks, Tamils and Sinhalese, Tibetans and Chinese, Japanese and Americans all belong to a single Western-defined universal civilization is to fly in the face of reality.

A universal civilization can only be the product of universal power. Roman power created a near-universal civilization within the limited confines of the ancient world. Western power in the form of European colonialism in the nineteenth century and American hegemony in the twentieth century extended Western culture throughout much of the contemporary world. European colonialism is over; American hegemony is receding. The erosion of Western culture follows, as indigenous, historically rooted mores, languages, beliefs and institutions reassert themselves.

Amazingly, Ajami cites India as evidence of the sweeping power of Western modernity. "India," he says, "will not become a Hindu state. The inheritance of Indian secularism will hold." Maybe it will, but certainly the overwhelming trend is away from Nehru's vision of a secular, socialist, Western, parliamentary democracy to a society shaped by Hindu fundamentalism. In India, Ajami goes on to say, "The vast middle class will defend it [secularism], keep the order intact to maintain India's—and its own—place in the modern world of nations." Really? A long *New York Times* (September 23, 1993) story on this subject begins: "Slowly, gradually, but with the relentlessness of floodwaters, a growing Hindu rage toward India's Muslim minority has been spreading among India's solid middle class Hindus—its merchants and accountants, its lawyers and engineers—creating uncertainty about the future ability of adherents of the two religions to get along." An op-ed piece in the *Times* (August 3, 1993) by an Indian journalist also highlights the role of the middle class: "The most disturbing development is the increasing number of senior civil servants, intellectuals, and journalists who have begun to talk the language of Hindu fundamentalism, protesting that religious minorities, particularly the Muslims, have pushed them beyond the limits of patience." This author, Khushwant Singh, concludes sadly that while India may retain a secular facade, India "will no longer be the India we have known over the past 47 years" and "the spirit within will be that of militant Hinduism." In India, as in other societies, fundamentalism is on the rise and is largely a middle class phenomenon.

The decline of Western power will be followed, and is beginning to be followed, by the retreat of Western culture. The rapidly increasing economic power of East Asian states will, as Kishore Mahbubani asserted, lead to increasing military power, political influence and cultural assertiveness. A colleague of his has elaborated this warning with respect to human rights:

[E]fforts to promote human rights in Asia must also reckon with the altered distribution of power in the post-Cold War world. . . . Western leverage over East and Southeast Asia has been greatly reduced. . . . There is far less scope for conditionality and sanctions to force compliance with human rights. . . .

For the first time since the Universal Declaration [on Human Rights] was adopted in 1948, countries not thoroughly steeped in the Judeo-Christian and natural law traditions are in the first rank: That unprecedented situation will define the new international politics of human rights. It will also multiply the occasions for conflict. . . .

Economic success has engendered a greater cultural self-confidence. Whatever their differences, East and Southeast Asian countries are increasingly conscious of their own civilizations and tend to locate the sources of their economic success in their own distinctive traditions and institutions. The self-congratulatory, simplistic, and sanctimonious tone of much Western commentary at the end of the Cold War and the current triumphalism of Western values grate on East and Southeast Asians.[3]

Language is, of course, central to culture, and Ajami and Robert Bartley both cite the widespread use of English as evidence for the universality of Western culture (although Ajami's fictional example dates from 1900). Is, however, use of English increasing or decreasing in relation to other languages? In India, Africa and elsewhere, indigenous languages have been replacing those of the colonial rulers. Even as Ajami and Bartley were penning their comments, *Newsweek* ran an article entitled "English Not Spoken Here Much Anymore" on Chinese replacing English as the lingua franca of Hong Kong.[4] In a parallel development, Serbs now call their language Serbian, not Serbo-Croatian, and write it in the Cyrillic script of their Russian kinsmen, not in the Western script of their Catholic enemies. At the same time, Azerbaijan, Turkmenistan, and Uzbekistan have shifted from the Cyrillic script of their former Russian masters to the Western script of their Turkish kinsmen. On the language front, Babelization prevails over universalization and further evidences the rise of civilization identity.

CULTURE IS TO DIE FOR

Wherever one turns, the world is at odds with itself. If differences in civilization are not responsible for these conflicts,

---

[3]Bilahari Kausikan, "Asia's Different Standard," *Foreign Policy*, Fall 1993, pp. 28-34. In an accompanying article Aryeh Neier excoriates "Asia's Unacceptable Standard," ibid., pp. 42-51.

[4]In the words of one British resident: "When I arrived in Hong Kong 10 years ago, nine times out of 10, a taxi driver would understand where you were going. Now, nine times out of 10, he doesn't." Occidentals rather than natives increasingly have to be hired to fill jobs requiring knowledge of English. *Newsweek*, July 19, 1993, p. 24.

what is? The critics of the civilization paradigm have not produced a better explanation for what is going on in the world. The civilizational paradigm, in contrast, strikes a responsive chord throughout the world. In Asia, as one U.S. ambassador reported, it is "spreading like wildfire." In Europe, European Community President Jacques Delors explicitly endorsed its argument that "future conflicts will be sparked by cultural factors rather than economics or ideology" and warned, "The West needs to develop a deeper understanding of the religious and philosophical assumptions underlying other civilizations, and the way other nations see their interests, to identify what we have in common." Muslims, in turn, have seen "the clash" as providing recognition and, in some degree, legitimation for the distinctiveness of their own civilization and its independence from the West. That civilizations are meaningful entities accords with the way in which people see and experience reality.

History has not ended. The world is not one. Civilizations unite and divide humankind. The forces making for clashes between civilizations can be contained only if they are recognized. In a "world of different civilizations," as my article concluded, each "will have to learn to coexist with the others." What ultimately counts for people is not political ideology or economic interest. Faith and family, blood and belief, are what people identify with and what they will fight and die for. And that is why the clash of civilizations is replacing the Cold War as the central phenomenon of global politics, and why a civilizational paradigm provides, better than any alternative, a useful starting point for understanding and coping with the changes going on in the world.

Clash of Globalizations

Stanley Hoffmann

JULY/AUGUST 2002

A NEW PARADIGM?

What is the state of international relations today? In the 1990s, specialists concentrated on the partial disintegration of the global order's traditional foundations: states. During that decade, many countries, often those born of decolonization, revealed themselves to be no more than pseudostates, without solid institutions, internal cohesion, or national consciousness. The end of communist coercion in the former Soviet Union and in the former Yugoslavia also revealed long-hidden ethnic tensions. Minorities that were or considered themselves oppressed demanded independence. In Iraq, Sudan, Afghanistan, and Haiti, rulers waged open warfare against their subjects. These wars increased the importance of humanitarian interventions, which came at the expense of the hallowed principles of national sovereignty and nonintervention. Thus the dominant tension of the decade was the clash between the fragmentation of states (and the state system) and the progress of economic, cultural, and political integration—in other words, globalization.

Everybody has understood the events of September 11 as the beginning of a new era. But what does this break mean? In the conventional approach to international relations, war took

STANLEY HOFFMANN is Buttenwieser University Professor at Harvard University and a regular book reviewer for *Foreign Affairs*.

place among states. But in September, poorly armed individuals suddenly challenged, surprised, and wounded the world's dominant superpower. The attacks also showed that, for all its accomplishments, globalization makes an awful form of violence easily accessible to hopeless fanatics. Terrorism is the bloody link between interstate relations and global society. As countless individuals and groups are becoming global actors along with states, insecurity and vulnerability are rising. To assess today's bleak state of affairs, therefore, several questions are necessary. What concepts help explain the new global order? What is the condition of the interstate part of international relations? And what does the emerging global civil society contribute to world order?

SOUND AND FURY

Two models made a great deal of noise in the 1990s. The first one—Francis Fukuyama's "End of History" thesis—was not vindicated by events. To be sure, his argument predicted the end of ideological conflicts, not history itself, and the triumph of political and economic liberalism. That point is correct in a narrow sense: the "secular religions" that fought each other so bloodily in the last century are now dead. But Fukuyama failed to note that nationalism remains very much alive. Moreover, he ignored the explosive potential of religious wars that has extended to a large part of the Islamic world.

Fukuyama's academic mentor, the political scientist Samuel Huntington, provided a few years later a gloomier account that saw a very different world. Huntington predicted that violence resulting from international anarchy and the absence of common values and institutions would erupt among civilizations rather than among states or ideologies. But Huntington's conception of what constitutes a civilization was hazy. He failed to take into account sufficiently conflicts within each so-called civilization, and he overestimated the importance of religion in the behavior of non-Western elites, who are often secularized and Westernized. Hence he could not clearly define the link between a civilization and the foreign policies of its member states.

Other, less sensational models still have adherents. The "realist" orthodoxy insists that nothing has changed in international relations since Thucydides and Machiavelli: a state's military and economic power determines its fate; interdependence and international institutions are secondary and fragile phenomena; and states' objectives are imposed by the threats to their survival or security. Such is the world described by Henry Kissinger. Unfortunately, this venerable model has trouble integrating change, especially globalization and the rise of nonstate actors. Moreover, it overlooks the need for international cooperation that results from such new threats as the proliferation of weapons of mass destruction (WMD). And it ignores what the scholar Raymond Aron called the "germ of a universal consciousness": the liberal, promarket norms that developed states have come to hold in common.

Taking Aron's point, many scholars today interpret the world in terms of a triumphant globalization that submerges borders through new means of information and communication. In this universe, a state choosing to stay closed invariably faces decline and growing discontent among its subjects, who are eager for material progress. But if it opens up, it must accept a reduced role that is mainly limited to social protection, physical protection against aggression or civil war, and maintaining national identity. The champion of this epic without heroes is *The New York Times* columnist Thomas Friedman. He contrasts barriers with open vistas, obsolescence with modernity, state control with free markets. He sees in globalization the light of dawn, the "golden straitjacket" that will force contentious publics to understand that the logic of globalization is that of peace (since war would interrupt globalization and therefore progress) and democracy (because new technologies increase individual autonomy and encourage initiative).

BACK TO REALITY

These models come up hard against three realities. First, rivalries among great powers (and the capacity of smaller states to exploit such tensions) have most certainly not disappeared. For a while now, however, the existence of nuclear weapons has produced a certain degree of prudence among the powers that have them. The risk of destruction that these weapons hold has moderated the game and turned nuclear arms into instruments of last resort. But the game could heat up as more states seek other WMD as a way of narrowing the gap between the nuclear club and the other powers. The sale of such weapons thus becomes a hugely contentious issue, and efforts to slow down the spread of all WMD, especially to dangerous "rogue" states, can paradoxically become new causes of violence.

Second, if wars between states are becoming less common, wars within them are on the rise—as seen in the former Yugoslavia, Iraq, much of Africa, and Sri Lanka. Uninvolved states first tend to hesitate to get engaged in these complex conflicts, but they then (sometimes) intervene to prevent these conflicts from turning into regional catastrophes. The interveners, in turn, seek the help of the United Nations or regional organizations to rebuild these states, promote stability, and prevent future fragmentation and misery.

Third, states' foreign policies are shaped not only by realist geopolitical factors such as economics and military power but by domestic politics. Even in undemocratic regimes, forces such as xenophobic passions, economic grievances, and transnational ethnic solidarity can make policymaking far more complex and less predictable. Many states—especially the United States—have to grapple with the frequent interplay of competing government branches. And the importance of individual leaders and their personalities is often underestimated in the study of international affairs.

For realists, then, transnational terrorism creates a formidable dilemma. If a state is the victim of private actors such as terrorists, it will try to eliminate these groups by depriving them of sanctuaries and punishing the states that harbor them. The national interest of the attacked state will therefore require either armed interventions against governments supporting terrorists or a course of prudence and discreet pressure on other governments to bring these terrorists to justice. Either option requires a questioning of sovereignty—the holy concept of realist theories. The classical realist universe of Hans Morgenthau and Aron may therefore still be very much alive in a world of states, but it has increasingly hazy contours and offers only difficult choices when it faces the threat of terrorism.

At the same time, the real universe of globalization does not resemble the one that Friedman celebrates. In fact, globalization has three forms, each with its own problems. First is economic globalization, which results from recent revolutions in technology, information, trade, foreign investment, and international business. The main actors are companies, investors, banks, and private services industries, as well as states and international organizations. This present form of capitalism, ironically foreseen by Karl Marx and Friedrich Engels, poses a central dilemma between efficiency and fairness. The specialization and integration of firms make it possible to increase aggregate wealth, but the logic of pure capitalism does not favor social justice. Economic globalization has thus become a formidable cause of inequality among and within states, and the concern for global competitiveness limits the aptitude of states and other actors to address this problem.

Next comes cultural globalization. It stems from the technological revolution and economic globalization, which together foster the flow of cultural goods. Here the key choice is between uniformization (often termed "Americanization") and diversity. The result is both a "disenchantment of the world" (in Max Weber's words) and a reaction against uniformity. The latter takes form in a renaissance of local cultures and languages as well as assaults against Western culture, which is denounced as an arrogant bearer of a secular, revolutionary ideology and a mask for U.S. hegemony.

Finally there is political globalization, a product of the other two. It is characterized by the preponderance of the United States and its political institutions and by a vast array of international and regional organizations and transgovernmental networks (specializing in areas such as policing or migration or justice). It is also marked by private institutions that are neither governmental nor purely national—say, Doctors Without Borders or Amnesty International. But many of these agencies lack democratic accountability and are weak in scope, power, and authority. Furthermore, much uncertainty hangs over the fate of American hegemony, which faces significant resistance abroad and is affected by America's own oscillation between the temptations of domination and isolation.

The benefits of globalization are undeniable. But Friedmanlike optimism rests on very fragile foundations. For one thing, globalization is neither inevitable nor irresistible. Rather, it is largely an American creation, rooted in the period after World War II and based on U.S. economic might. By extension, then, a deep and protracted economic crisis in the United States could have as devastating an effect on globalization as did the Great Depression.

Second, globalization's reach remains limited because it excludes many poor countries, and the states that it does transform react in different ways. This fact stems from the diversity of economic and social conditions at home as well as from partisan politics. The world is far away from a perfect integration of markets, services, and factors of production. Sometimes the simple existence of borders slows down and can even paralyze this integration; at other times it gives integration the flavors and colors of the dominant state (as in the case of the Internet).

Third, international civil society remains embryonic. Many nongovernmental organizations reflect only a tiny segment of the populations of their members' states. They largely represent only modernized countries, or those in which the weight of the state is not too heavy. Often, NGOs have little independence from governments.

Fourth, the individual emancipation so dear to Friedman does not quickly succeed in democratizing regimes, as one can see today in China. Nor does emancipation prevent public institutions such as the International Monetary Fund, the World Bank, or the World Trade Organization from remaining opaque in their activities and often arbitrary and unfair in their rulings.

Fifth, the attractive idea of improving the human condition through the abolition of barriers is dubious. Globalization is in fact only a sum of techniques (audio and videocassettes, the Internet, instantaneous communications) that are at the disposal of states or private actors. Self-interest and ideology, not humanitarian reasons, are what drive these actors. Their behavior is quite different from the vision of globalization as an Enlightenment-based utopia that is simultaneously scientific, rational, and universal. For many reasons—misery, injustice, humiliation, attachment to traditions, aspiration to more than just a better standard of living—this "Enlightenment" stereotype of globalization thus provokes revolt and dissatisfaction.

Another contradiction is also at work. On the one hand, international and transnational cooperation is necessary to ensure that globalization will not be undermined by the inequalities resulting from market fluctuations, weak state-sponsored protections, and the incapacity of many states to improve their fates by themselves. On the other hand, cooperation presupposes that many states and rich private players operate altruistically—which is certainly not the essence of international relations—or practice a remarkably generous conception of their long-term interests. But the fact remains that most rich states still refuse to provide sufficient development aid or to intervene in crisis situations such as the genocide in Rwanda. That reluctance compares poorly with the American enthusiasm to pursue the fight against al Qaeda and the Taliban. What is wrong here is not patriotic enthusiasm as such, but the weakness of the humanitarian impulse when the national interest in saving non-American victims is not self-evident.

IMAGINED COMMUNITIES

Among the many effects of globalization on international politics, three hold particular importance. The first concerns institutions. Contrary to realist predictions, most states are not perpetually at war with each other. Many regions and countries live in peace; in other cases, violence is internal rather than state-to-state. And since no government can do everything by itself, interstate organisms have emerged. The result, which can be termed "global society," seeks to reduce the potentially destructive effects of national regulations on the forces of integration. But it also seeks to ensure fairness in the world market and create international regulatory regimes in such areas as trade, communications, human rights, migration, and refugees. The main obstacle to this effort is the reluctance of states to accept global directives that might constrain the market or further reduce their sovereignty. Thus the UN's powers remain limited and sometimes only purely theoretical. International criminal justice is still only a spotty and contested last resort. In the world economy—where the market, not global governance, has been the main beneficiary of the state's retreat—the network of global institutions is fragmented and incomplete. Foreign investment remains ruled by bilateral agreements. Environmental protection is badly ensured, and issues such as migration and population growth are largely ignored. Institutional networks are not powerful enough to address unfettered short-term capital movements, the lack of international regulation on bankruptcy and competition, and primitive coordination among rich countries. In turn, the global "governance" that does exist is partial and weak at a time when economic globalization deprives many states of independent monetary and fiscal policies, or it obliges them to make cruel choices between economic competitiveness and the preservation of social safety nets. All the while, the United States displays an increasing impatience toward institutions that weigh on American freedom of action. Movement toward a world state looks increasingly unlikely. The more state sovereignty crumbles under the blows of globalization or such recent developments as humanitarian intervention and the fight against terrorism, the more states cling to what is left to them.

Second, globalization has not profoundly challenged the enduring national nature of citizenship. Economic life takes place on a global scale, but human identity remains national—hence the strong resistance to cultural homogenization. Over the centuries, increasingly centralized states have expanded their functions and tried to forge a sense of common identity for their subjects. But no central power in the world can do the same thing today, even in the European Union. There, a single currency and advanced economic coordination have not yet produced a unified economy or strong central institutions endowed with legal autonomy, nor have they resulted in a sense of postnational citizenship. The march from national identity to one that would be both national and European has only just begun. A world very partially unified by technology still has no collective consciousness or collective solidarity. What states are unwilling to do the world market cannot do all by itself, especially in engendering a sense of world citizenship.

Third, there is the relationship between globalization and violence. The traditional state of war, even if it is limited in scope, still persists. There are high risks of regional explosions in the Middle East and in East Asia, and these could seriously affect relations between the major powers. Because of this threat, and because modern arms are increasingly costly, the "anarchical society" of states lacks the resources to correct some of globalization's most flagrant flaws. These very costs, combined with the classic distrust among international actors who prefer to try to preserve their security alone or through traditional alliances, prevent a more satisfactory institutionalization of world politics—for example, an increase of the UN's powers. This step could happen if global society were provided with sufficient forces to prevent a conflict or restore peace—but it is not.

Globalization, far from spreading peace, thus seems to foster conflicts and resentments. The lowering of various barriers celebrated by Friedman, especially the spread of global media, makes it possible for the most deprived or oppressed to compare their fate with that of the free and well-off. These dispossessed then ask for help from others with common resentments, ethnic origin, or religious faith. Insofar as globalization enriches some and uproots many, those who are both poor and uprooted may seek revenge and self-esteem in terrorism.

GLOBALIZATION AND TERROR

Terrorism is the poisoned fruit of several forces. It can be the weapon of the weak in a classic conflict among states or within a state, as in Kashmir or the Palestinian territories. But it can also be seen as a product of globalization. Transnational terrorism is made possible by the vast array of communication tools. Islamic terrorism, for example, is not only based on support for the Palestinian struggle and opposition to an invasive American presence. It is also fueled by a resistance to "unjust" economic globalization and to a Western culture deemed threatening to local religions and cultures.

If globalization often facilitates terrorist violence, the fight against this war without borders is potentially disastrous for both economic development and globalization. Antiterrorist measures restrict mobility and financial flows, while new terrorist attacks could lead the way for an antiglobalist reaction comparable to the chauvinistic paroxysms of the 1930s. Global terrorism is not the simple extension of war among states to nonstates. It is the subversion of traditional ways of war because it does not care about the sovereignty of either its enemies or the allies who shelter them. It provokes its victims to take measures that, in the name of legitimate defense, violate knowingly the sovereignty of those states accused of encouraging terror. (After all, it was not the Taliban's infamous domestic violations of human rights that led the United States into Afghanistan; it was the Taliban's support of Osama bin Laden.)

But all those trespasses against the sacred principles of sovereignty do not constitute progress toward global society, which has yet to agree on a common definition of terrorism or on a common policy against it. Indeed, the beneficiaries of the antiterrorist "war" have been the illiberal, poorer states that have lost so much of their sovereignty of late. Now the crackdown on terror allows them to tighten their controls on their own people, products, and money. They can give themselves new reasons to violate individual rights in the name of common defense against insecurity—and thus stop the slow, hesitant march toward international criminal justice.

Another main beneficiary will be the United States, the only actor capable of carrying the war against terrorism into all corners of the world. Despite its power, however, America cannot fully protect itself against future terrorist acts, nor can it fully overcome its ambivalence toward forms of interstate cooperation that might restrict U.S. freedom of action. Thus terrorism is a global phenomenon that ultimately reinforces the enemy— the state—at the same time as it tries to destroy it. The states that are its targets have no interest in applying the laws of war to their fight against terrorists; they have every interest in treating terrorists as outlaws and pariahs. The champions of globalization have sometimes glimpsed the "jungle" aspects of economic globalization, but few observers foresaw similar aspects in global terrorist and antiterrorist violence.

Finally, the unique position of the United States raises a serious question over the future of world affairs. In the realm of interstate problems, American behavior will determine whether the nonsuperpowers and weak states will continue to look at the United States as a friendly power (or at least a tolerable hegemon), or whether they are provoked by Washington's hubris into coalescing against American preponderance. America may be a hegemon, but combining rhetorical overkill and ill-defined designs is full of risks. Washington has yet to understand that nothing is more dangerous for a "hyperpower" than the temptation of unilateralism. It may well believe that the constraints of international agreements and organizations are not necessary, since U.S. values and power are all that is needed for world order. But in reality, those same international constraints provide far better opportunities for leadership than arrogant demonstrations of contempt for others' views, and they offer useful ways of restraining unilateralist behavior in other states. A hegemon concerned with prolonging its rule should be especially interested in using internationalist methods and institutions, for the gain in influence far exceeds the loss in freedom of action.

In the realm of global society, much will depend on whether the United States will overcome its frequent indifference to the costs that globalization imposes on poorer countries. For now, Washington is too reluctant to make resources available for economic development, and it remains hostile to agencies that monitor and regulate the global market. All too often, the right-leaning tendencies of the American political system push U.S. diplomacy toward an excessive reliance on America's greatest asset—military strength—as well as an excessive reliance on market capitalism and a "sovereigntism" that offends and alienates. That the mighty United States is so afraid of the world's imposing its "inferior" values on Americans is often a source of ridicule and indignation abroad.

ODD MAN OUT

For all these tensions, it is still possible that the American war on terrorism will be contained by prudence, and that other governments will give priority to the many internal problems created by interstate rivalries and the flaws of globalization. But the world risks being squeezed between a new Scylla and Charybdis. The Charybdis is universal intervention, unilaterally decided by American leaders who are convinced that they have found a global mission provided by a colossal threat. Presentable as an epic contest between good and evil, this struggle offers the best way of rallying the population and overcoming domestic divisions. The Scylla is resignation to universal chaos in the form of new attacks by future bin Ladens, fresh humanitarian disasters, or regional wars that risk escalation. Only through wise judgment can the path between them be charted.

We can analyze the present, but we cannot predict the future. We live in a world where a society of uneven and often virtual states overlaps with a global society burdened by weak public institutions and underdeveloped civil society. A single power dominates, but its economy could become unmanageable or distrusted by future terrorist attacks. Thus to predict the future confidently would be highly incautious or naive. To be sure, the world has survived many crises, but it has done so at a very high price, even in times when WMD were not available.

Precisely because the future is neither decipherable nor determined, students of international relations face two missions. They must try to understand what goes on by taking an inventory of current goods and disentangling the threads of present networks. But the fear of confusing the empirical with the normative should not prevent them from writing as political philosophers at a time when many philosophers are extending their conceptions of just society to international relations. How can one make the global house more livable? The answer presupposes a political philosophy that would be both just and acceptable even to those whose values have other foundations. As the late philosopher Judith Shklar did, we can take as a point of departure and as a guiding thread the fate of the victims of violence, oppression, and misery; as a goal, we should seek material and moral emancipation. While taking into account the formidable constraints of the world as it is, it is possible to loosen them.

Us and Them

The Enduring Power of Ethnic Nationalism

Jerry Z. Muller

MARCH/APRIL 2008

Projecting their own experience onto the rest of the world, Americans generally belittle the role of ethnic nationalism in politics. After all, in the United States people of varying ethnic origins live cheek by jowl in relative peace. Within two or three generations of immigration, their ethnic identities are attenuated by cultural assimilation and intermarriage. Surely, things cannot be so different elsewhere.

Americans also find ethnonationalism discomfiting both intellectually and morally. Social scientists go to great lengths to demonstrate that it is a product not of nature but of culture, often deliberately constructed. And ethicists scorn value systems based on narrow group identities rather than cosmopolitanism.

But none of this will make ethnonationalism go away. Immigrants to the united states usually arrive with a willingness to fit into their new country and reshape their identities accordingly. But for those who remain behind in lands where their ancestors have lived for generations, if not centuries, political identities often take ethnic form, producing competing communal claims to political power. The creation of a peaceful regional

JERRY Z. MULLER is Professor of History at the Catholic University of America. His most recent book is *The Mind and the Market: Capitalism in Modern European Thought.*

order of nation-states has usually been the product of a violent process of ethnic separation. In areas where that separation has not yet occurred, politics is apt to remain ugly.

A familiar and influential narrative of twentieth-century European history argues that nationalism twice led to war, in 1914 and then again in 1939. Thereafter, the story goes, Europeans concluded that nationalism was a danger and gradually abandoned it. In the postwar decades, western Europeans enmeshed themselves in a web of transnational institutions, culminating in the European Union (EU). After the fall of the Soviet empire, that transnational framework spread eastward to encompass most of the continent. Europeans entered a postnational era, which was not only a good thing in itself but also a model for other regions. Nationalism, in this view, had been a tragic detour on the road to a peaceful liberal democratic order.

This story is widely believed by educated Europeans and even more so, perhaps, by educated Americans. Recently, for example, in the course of arguing that Israel ought to give up its claim to be a Jewish state and dissolve itself into some sort of binational entity with the Palestinians, the prominent historian Tony Judt informed the readers of *The New York Review of Books* that "the problem with Israel . . . [is that] it has imported a characteristically late-nineteenth-century separatist project into a world that has moved on, a world of individual rights, open frontiers, and international law. The very idea of a 'Jewish state' . . . is an anachronism."

Yet the experience of the hundreds of Africans and Asians who perish each year trying to get into Europe by landing on the coast of Spain or Italy reveals that Europe's frontiers are not so open. And a survey would show that whereas in 1900 there were many states in Europe without a single overwhelmingly dominant nationality, by 2007 there were only two, and one of those, Belgium, was close to breaking up. Aside from Switzerland, in other words—where the domestic ethnic balance of power is protected by strict citizenship laws—in Europe the "separatist project" has not so much vanished as triumphed.

Far from having been superannuated in 1945, in many respects ethnonationalism was at its apogee in the years immediately after World War II. European stability during the Cold War era was in fact due partly to the widespread fulfillment of the ethnonationalist project. And since the end of the Cold War, ethnonationalism has continued to reshape European borders.

In short, ethnonationalism has played a more profound and lasting role in modern history than is commonly understood, and the processes that led to the dominance of the ethnonational state and the separation of ethnic groups in Europe are likely to reoccur elsewhere. Increased urbanization, literacy, and political mobilization; differences in the fertility rates and economic performance of various ethnic groups; and immigration will challenge the internal structure of states as well as their borders. Whether politically correct or not, ethnonationalism will continue to shape the world in the twenty-first century.

THE POLITICS OF IDENTITY

There are two major ways of thinking about national identity. One is that all people who live within a country's borders are part of the nation, regardless of their ethnic, racial, or religious origins. This liberal or civic nationalism is the conception with which contemporary Americans are most likely to identify. But the liberal view has competed with and often lost out to a different view, that of ethnonationalism. The core of the ethnonationalist idea is that nations are defined by a shared heritage, which usually includes a common language, a common faith, and a common ethnic ancestry.

The ethnonationalist view has traditionally dominated through much of Europe and has held its own even in the United States until recently. For substantial stretches of U.S.

history, it was believed that only the people of English origin, or those who were Protestant, or white, or hailed from northern Europe were real Americans. It was only in 1965 that the reform of U.S. immigration law abolished the system of national-origin quotas that had been in place for several decades. This system had excluded Asians entirely and radically restricted immigration from southern and eastern Europe.

Ethnonationalism draws much of its emotive power from the notion that the members of a nation are part of an extended family, ultimately united by ties of blood. It is the subjective belief in the reality of a common "we" that counts. The markers that distinguish the in-group vary from case to case and time to time, and the subjective nature of the communal boundaries has led some to discount their practical significance. But as Walker Connor, an astute student of nationalism, has noted, "It is not what is, but what people believe is that has behavioral consequences." And the central tenets of ethnonationalist belief are that nations exist, that each nation ought to have its own state, and that each state should be made up of the members of a single nation.

The conventional narrative of European history asserts that nationalism was primarily liberal in the western part of the continent and that it became more ethnically oriented as one moved east. There is some truth to this, but it disguises a good deal as well. It is more accurate to say that when modern states began to form, political boundaries and ethnolinguistic boundaries largely coincided in the areas along Europe's Atlantic coast. Liberal nationalism, that is, was most apt to emerge in states that already possessed a high degree of ethnic homogeneity. Long before the nineteenth century, countries such as England, France, Portugal, Spain, and Sweden emerged as nation-states in polities where ethnic divisions had been softened by a long history of cultural and social homogenization.

In the center of the continent, populated by speakers of

German and Italian, political structures were fragmented into hundreds of small units. But in the 1860s and 1870s, this fragmentation was resolved by the creation of Italy and Germany, so that almost all Italians lived in the former and a majority of Germans lived in the latter. Moving further east, the situation changed again. As late as 1914, most of central, eastern, and southeastern Europe was made up not of nation-states but of empires. The Hapsburg empire comprised what are now Austria, the Czech Republic, Hungary, and Slovakia and parts of what are now Bosnia, Croatia, Poland, Romania, Ukraine, and more. The Romanov empire stretched into Asia, including what is now Russia and what are now parts of Poland, Ukraine, and more. And the Ottoman Empire covered modern Turkey and parts of today's Bulgaria, Greece, Romania, and Serbia and extended through much of the Middle East and North Africa as well.

Each of these empires was composed of numerous ethnic groups, but they were not multinational in the sense of granting equal status to the many peoples that made up their populaces. The governing monarchy and landed nobility often differed in language and ethnic origin from the urbanized trading class, whose members in turn usually differed in language, ethnicity, and often religion from the peasantry. In the Hapsburg and Romanov empires, for example, merchants were usually Germans or Jews. In the Ottoman Empire, they were often Armenians, Greeks, or Jews. And in each empire, the peasantry was itself ethnically diverse.

Up through the nineteenth century, these societies were still largely agrarian: most people lived as peasants in the countryside, and few were literate. Political, social, and economic stratifications usually correlated with ethnicity, and people did not expect to change their positions in the system. Until the rise of modern nationalism, all of this seemed quite unproblematic. In this world, moreover, people of one religion, language, or culture were often dispersed across various countries and empires. There were ethnic Germans, for example, not only in the areas that became Germany but also scattered throughout the Hapsburg and Romanov empires. There were Greeks in Greece but also millions of them in the Ottoman Empire (not to mention hundreds of thousands of Muslim Turks in Greece). And there were Jews everywhere—but with no independent state of their own.

THE RISE OF ETHNONATIONALISM

Today, people tend to take the nation-state for granted as the natural form of political association and regard empires as anomalies. But over the broad sweep of recorded history, the opposite is closer to the truth. Most people at most times have lived in empires, with the nation-state the exception rather than the rule. So what triggered the change?

The rise of ethnonationalism, as the sociologist Ernest Gellner has explained, was not some strange historical mistake; rather, it was propelled by some of the deepest currents of modernity. Military competition between states created a demand for expanded state resources and hence continual economic growth. Economic growth, in turn, depended on mass literacy and easy communication, spurring policies to promote education and a common language—which led directly to conflicts over language and communal opportunities.

Modern societies are premised on the egalitarian notion that in theory, at least, anyone can aspire to any economic position. But in practice, everyone does not have an equal likelihood of upward economic mobility, and not simply because individuals have different innate capabilities. For such advances depend in part on what economists call "cultural capital, " the skills and behavioral patterns that help individuals and groups succeed. Groups with traditions of literacy and engagement in commerce tend to excel, for example, whereas those without such traditions tend to lag behind.

As they moved into cities and got more education during the nineteenth and early twentieth centuries, ethnic groups with largely peasant backgrounds, such as the Czechs, the Poles, the Slovaks, and the Ukrainians found that key positions in the government and the economy were already occupied—often by ethnic Armenians, Germans, Greeks, or Jews. Speakers of the same language came to share a sense that they belonged together and to define themselves in contrast to other communities. And eventually they came to demand a nationstate of their own, in which they would be the masters, dominating politics, staffing the civil service, and controlling commerce.

Ethnonationalism had a psychological basis as well as an economic one. By creating a new and direct relationship between individuals and the government, the rise of the modern state weakened individuals' traditional bonds to intermediate social units, such as the family, the clan, the guild, and the church. And by spurring social and geographic mobility and a self-help mentality, the rise of market-based economies did the same. The result was an emotional vacuum that was often filled by new forms of identification, often along ethnic lines.

Ethnonationalist ideology called for a congruence between the state and the ethnically defined nation, with explosive results. As Lord Acton recognized in 1862, "By making the state and the nation commensurate with each other in theory, [nationalism] reduces practically to a subject condition all other nationalities that may be within the boundary. . . . According, therefore, to the degree of humanity and civilization in that dominant body which claims all the rights of the community, the inferior races are exterminated, or reduced to servitude, or outlawed, or put in a condition of dependence." And that is just what happened.

Jerry Z. Muller

THE GREAT TRANSFORMATION

Nineteenth-century liberals, like many proponents of globalization today, believed that the spread of international commerce would lead people to recognize the mutual benefits that could come from peace and trade, both within polities and between them. Socialists agreed, although they believed that harmony would come only after the arrival of socialism. Yet that was not the course that twentieth-century history was destined to follow. The process of "making the state and the nation commensurate" took a variety of forms, from voluntary emigration (often motivated by governmental discrimination against minority ethnicities) to forced deportation (also known as "population transfer") to genocide. Although the term "ethnic cleansing" has come into English usage only recently, its verbal correlates in Czech, French, German, and Polish go back much further. Much of the history of twentieth-century Europe, in fact, has been a painful, drawn-out process of ethnic disaggregation.

Massive ethnic disaggregation began on Europe's frontiers. In the ethnically mixed Balkans, wars to expand the nation-states of Bulgaria, Greece, and Serbia at the expense of the ailing Ottoman Empire were accompanied by ferocious inter-ethnic violence. During the Balkan Wars of 1912-13, almost half a million people left their traditional homelands, either voluntarily or by force. Muslims left regions under the control of Bulgarians, Greeks, and Serbs; Bulgarians abandoned Greek-controlled areas of Macedonia; Greeks fled from regions of Macedonia ceded to Bulgaria and Serbia.

World War I led to the demise of the three great turn-of-the-century empires, unleashing an explosion of ethnonationalism in the process. In the Ottoman Empire, mass deportations and murder during the war took the lives of a million members of the local Armenian minority in an early attempt at

ethnic cleansing, if not genocide. In 1919, the Greek government invaded the area that would become Turkey, seeking to
carve out a "greater Greece" stretching all the way to Constantinople. Meeting with initial success, the Greek forces looted
and burned villages in an effort to drive out the region's ethnic
Turks. But Turkish forces eventually regrouped and pushed
the Greek army back, engaging in their own ethnic cleansing
against local Greeks along the way. Then the process of population transfers was formalized in the 1923 Treaty of Lausanne:
all ethnic Greeks were to go to Greece, all Greek Muslims to
Turkey. In the end, Turkey expelled almost 1.5 million people,
and Greece expelled almost 400, 000.

Out of the breakup of the Hapsburg and Romanov empires
emerged a multitude of new countries. Many conceived of
themselves as ethnonational polities, in which the state existed
to protect and promote the dominant ethnic group. Yet of central and eastern Europe's roughly 60 million people, 25 million
continued to be part of ethnic minorities in the countries in
which they lived. In most cases, the ethnic majority did not
believe in trying to help minorities assimilate, nor were the
minorities always eager to do so themselves. Nationalist governments openly discriminated in favor of the dominant community. Government activities were conducted solely in the
language of the majority, and the civil service was reserved for
those who spoke it.

In much of central and eastern Europe, Jews had long played
an important role in trade and commerce. When they were
given civil rights in the late nineteenth century, they tended to
excel in professions requiring higher education, such as medi-
cine and law, and soon Jews or people of Jewish descent made up
almost half the doctors and lawyers in cities such as Budapest,
Vienna, and Warsaw. By the 1930s, many governments adopted
policies to try to check and reverse these advances, denying Jews
credit and limiting their access to higher education. In other

words, the National Socialists who came to power in Germany in 1933 and based their movement around a "Germanness" they defined in contrast to "Jewishness" were an extreme version of a more common ethnonationalist trend.

The politics of ethnonationalism took an even deadlier turn during World War II. The Nazi regime tried to reorder the ethnic map of the continent by force. Its most radical act was an attempt to rid Europe of Jews by killing them all—an attempt that largely succeeded. The Nazis also used ethnic German minorities in Czechoslovakia, Poland, and elsewhere to enforce Nazi domination, and many of the regimes allied with Germany engaged in their own campaigns against internal ethnic enemies. The Romanian regime, for example, murdered hundreds of thousands of Jews on its own, without orders from Germany, and the government of Croatia murdered not only its Jews but hundreds of thousands of Serbs and Romany as well.

POSTWAR BUT NOT POSTNATIONAL

One might have expected that the Nazi regime's deadly policies and crushing defeat would mark the end of the ethnonationalist era. But in fact they set the stage for another massive round of ethnonational transformation. The political settlement in central Europe after World War I had been achieved primarily by moving borders to align them with populations. After World War II, it was the populations that moved instead. Millions of people were expelled from their homes and countries, with at least the tacit support of the victorious Allies.

Winston Churchill, Franklin Roosevelt, and Joseph Stalin all concluded that the expulsion of ethnic Germans from non-German countries was a prerequisite to a stable postwar order. As Churchill put it in a speech to the British parliament in December 1944, "Expulsion is the method which, so far as we have been able to see, will be the most satisfactory and lasting. There will be no mixture of populations to cause end-less trouble. . . . A clean sweep will be made. I am not alarmed at the prospect of the disentanglement of population, nor am I alarmed by these large transferences."He cited the Treaty of Lausanne as a precedent, showing how even the leaders of lib-eral democracies had concluded that only radically illiberal measures would eliminate the causes of ethnonational aspira-tions and aggression.

Between 1944 and 1945, five million ethnic Germans from the eastern parts of the German Reich fled westward to escape the conquering Red Army, which was energetically raping and massacring its way to Berlin. Then, between 1945 and 1947, the new postliberation regimes in Czechoslovakia, Hun-gary, Poland, and Yugoslavia expelled another seven million Germans in response to their collaboration with the Nazis. Together, these measures constituted the largest forced popula-tion movement in European history, with hundreds of thou-sands of people dying along the way.

The handful of Jews who survived the war and returned to their homes in eastern Europe met with so much anti-Semitism that most chose to leave for good. About 220, 000 of them made their way into the American-occupied zone of Germany, from which most eventually went to Israel or the United States. Jews thus essentially vanished from central and eastern Europe, which had been the center of Jewish life since the sixteenth century.

Millions of refugees from other ethnic groups were also evicted from their homes and resettled after the war. This was due partly to the fact that the borders of the Soviet Union had moved westward, into what had once been Poland, while the borders of Poland also moved westward, into what had once been Germany. To make populations correspond to the new borders, 1.5 million Poles living in areas that were now part of the Soviet Union were deported to Poland, and 500, 000 ethnic Ukrainians who had been living in Poland were sent to the Ukrainian Soviet Socialist Republic. Yet another exchange of populations took place between Czechoslovakia and Hungary, with Slovaks transferred out of Hungary and Magyars sent away from Czechoslovakia. A smaller number of Magyars also moved to Hungary from Yugoslavia, with Serbs and Croats moving in the opposite direction.

As a result of this massive process of ethnic unmixing, the ethnonationalist ideal was largely realized: for the most part, each nation in Europe had its own state, and each state was made up almost exclusively of a single ethnic nationality. During the Cold War, the few exceptions to this rule included Czechoslovakia, the Soviet Union, and Yugoslavia. But these countries' subsequent fate only demonstrated the ongoing vitality of ethnonationalism. After the fall of communism, East and West Germany were unified with remarkable rapidity, Czechoslovakia split peacefully into Czech and Slovak republics, and the Soviet Union broke apart into a variety of different national units. Since then, ethnic Russian minorities in many of the post-Soviet states have gradually immigrated to Russia, Magyars in Romania have moved to Hungary, and the few remaining ethnic Germans in Russia have largely gone to Germany. A million people of Jewish origin from the former Soviet Union have made their way to Israel. Yugoslavia saw the secession of Croatia and Slovenia and then descended into ethnonational wars over Bosnia and Kosovo.

The breakup of Yugoslavia was simply the last act of a long play. But the plot of that play—the disaggregation of peoples and the triumph of ethnonationalism in modern Europe—is rarely recognized, and so a story whose significance is comparable to the spread of democracy or capitalism remains largely unknown and unappreciated.

Us and Them

DECOLONIZATION AND AFTER

The effects of ethnonationalism, of course, have hardly been confined to Europe. For much of the developing world, decolonization has meant ethnic disaggregation through the exchange or expulsion of local minorities.

The end of the British Raj in 1947 brought about the partition of the subcontinent into India and Pakistan, along with an orgy of violence that took hundreds of thousands of lives. Fifteen million people became refugees, including Muslims who went to Pakistan and Hindus who went to India. Then, in 1971, Pakistan itself, originally unified on the basis of religion, dissolved into Urdu-speaking Pakistan and Bengali-speaking Bangladesh.

In the former British mandate of Palestine, a Jewish state was established in 1948 and was promptly greeted by the revolt of the indigenous Arab community and an invasion from the surrounding Arab states. In the war that resulted, regions that fell under Arab control were cleansed of their Jewish populations, and Arabs fled or were forced out of areas that came under Jewish control. Some 750, 000 Arabs left, primarily for the surrounding Arab countries, and the remaining 150, 000 constituted only about a sixth of the population of the new Jewish state. In the years afterward, nationalist-inspired violence against Jews in Arab countries propelled almost all of the more than 500, 000 Jews there to leave their lands of origin and immigrate to Israel. Likewise, in 1962 the end of French control in Algeria led to the forced emigration of Algerians of European origin (the so-called pieds-noirs), most of whom immigrated to France. Shortly thereafter, ethnic minorities of Asian origin were forced out of postcolonial Uganda. The legacy of the colonial era, moreover, is hardly finished. When the European overseas empires dissolved, they left behind a patchwork of states whose boundaries often cut across ethnic patterns of settlement and whose internal populations were ethnically mixed. It is wishful thinking to suppose that these boundaries will be permanent. As societies in the former colonial world modernize, becoming more urban, literate, and politically mobilized, the forces that gave rise to ethnonationalism and ethnic disaggregation in Europe are apt to drive events there, too.

THE BALANCE SHEET

Analysts of ethnic disaggregation typically focus on its destructive effects, which is understandable given the direct human suffering it has often entailed. But such attitudes can yield a distorted perspective by overlooking the less obvious costs and also the important benefits that ethnic separation has brought.

Economists from Adam Smith onward, for example, have argued that the efficiencies of competitive markets tend to increase with the markets' size. The dissolution of the Austro-Hungarian Empire into smaller nation-states, each with its own barriers to trade, was thus economically irrational and contributed to the region's travails in the interwar period. Much of subsequent European history has involved attempts to overcome this and other economic fragmentation, culminating in the EU.

Ethnic disaggregation also seems to have deleterious effects on cultural vitality. Precisely because most of their citizens share a common cultural and linguistic heritage, the homogenized states of postwar Europe have tended to be more culturally insular than their demographically diverse predecessors. With few Jews in Europe and few Germans in Prague, that is, there are fewer Franz Kafkas.

Forced migrations generally penalize the expelling countries and reward the receiving ones. Expulsion is often driven by a majority group's resentment of a minority group's success, on the mistaken assumption that achievement is a zero-sum game. But countries that got rid of their Armenians, Germans, Greeks, Jews, and other successful minorities deprived themselves of some of their most talented citizens, who simply took their skills and knowledge elsewhere. And in many places, the triumph of ethnonational politics has meant the victory of traditionally rural groups over more urbanized ones, which possess just those skills desirable in an advanced industrial economy.

But if ethnonationalism has frequently led to tension and conflict, it has also proved to be a source of cohesion and stability. When French textbooks began with "Our ancestors the Gauls" or when Churchill spoke to wartime audiences of "this island race," they appealed to ethnonationalist sensibilities as a source of mutual trust and sacrifice. Liberal democracy and ethnic homogeneity are not only compatible; they can be complementary.

One could argue that Europe has been so harmonious since World War II not because of the failure of ethnic nationalism but because of its success, which removed some of the greatest sources of conflict both within and between countries. The fact that ethnic and state boundaries now largely coincide has meant that there are fewer disputes over borders or expatriate communities, leading to the most stable territorial configuration in European history.

These ethnically homogeneous polities have displayed a great deal of internal solidarity, moreover, facilitating government programs, including domestic transfer payments, of various kinds. When the Swedish Social Democrats were developing plans for Europe's most extensive welfare state during the interwar period, the political scientist Sheri Berman has noted, they conceived of and sold them as the construction of a folkhemmet, or "people's home."

Several decades of life in consolidated, ethnically homogeneous states may even have worked to sap ethnonationalism's own emotional power. Many Europeans are now prepared, and even eager, to participate in transnational frameworks such as the EU, in part because their perceived need for collective self-determination has largely been satisfied.

NEW ETHNIC MIXING

Along with the process of forced ethnic disaggregation over the last two centuries, there has also been a process of ethnic mixing brought about by voluntary emigration. The general pattern has been one of emigration from poor, stagnant areas to richer and more dynamic ones.

In Europe, this has meant primarily movement west and north, leading above all to France and the United Kingdom. This pattern has continued into the present: as a result of recent migration, for example, there are now half a million Poles in Great Britain and 200, 000 in Ireland. Immigrants from one part of Europe who have moved to another and ended up staying there have tended to assimilate and, despite some grumbling about a supposed invasion of "Polish plumbers, " have created few significant problems.

The most dramatic transformation of European ethnic balances in recent decades has come from the immigration of people of Asian, African, and Middle Eastern origin, and here the results have been mixed. Some of these groups have achieved remarkable success, such as the Indian Hindus who have come to the United Kingdom. But in Belgium, France, Germany, the Netherlands, Sweden, the United Kingdom, and elsewhere, on balance the educational and economic progress of Muslim immigrants has been more limited and their cultural alienation greater.

How much of the problem can be traced to discrimination, how much to the cultural patterns of the immigrants themselves, and how much to the policies of European governments is difficult to determine. But a number of factors, from official multiculturalism to generous welfare states to the ease of contact with ethnic homelands, seem to have made it possible to create ethnic islands where assimilation into the larger culture and economy is limited.

As a result, some of the traditional contours of European politics have been upended. The left, for example, has tended to embrace immigration in the name of egalitarianism and multiculturalism. But if there is indeed a link between ethnic homogeneity and a population's willingness to support generous income-redistribution programs, the encouragement of a more heterogeneous society may end up undermining the left's broader political agenda. And some of Europe's libertarian cultural propensities have already clashed with the cultural illiberalism of some of the new immigrant communities.

Should Muslim immigrants not assimilate and instead develop a strong communal identification along religious lines, one consequence might be a resurgence of traditional ethnonational identities in some states—or the development of a new European identity defined partly in contradistinction to Islam (with the widespread resistance to the extension of full EU membership to Turkey being a possible harbinger of such a shift).

FUTURE IMPLICATIONS

Since ethnonationalism is a direct consequence of key elements of modernization, it is likely to gain ground in societies undergoing such a process. It is hardly surprising, therefore, that it remains among the most vital—and most disruptive—forces in many parts of the contemporary world.

More or less subtle forms of ethnonationalism, for example, are ubiquitous in immigration policy around the globe. Many countries—including Armenia, Bulgaria, Croatia, Finland,

Germany, Hungary, Ireland, Israel, Serbia, and Turkey—provide automatic or rapid citizenship to the members of diasporas of their own dominant ethnic group, if desired. Chinese immigration law gives priority and benefits to overseas Chinese. Portugal and Spain have immigration policies that favor applicants from their former colonies in the New World. Still other states, such as Japan and Slovakia, provide official forms of identification to members of the dominant national ethnic group who are noncitizens that permit them to live and work in the country. Americans, accustomed by the U.S. government's official practices to regard differential treatment on the basis of ethnicity to be a violation of universalist norms, often consider such policies exceptional, if not abhorrent. Yet in a global context, it is the insistence on universalist criteria that seems provincial.

Increasing communal consciousness and shifting ethnic balances are bound to have a variety of consequences, both within and between states, in the years to come. As economic globalization brings more states into the global economy, for example, the first fruits of that process will often fall to those ethnic groups best positioned by history or culture to take advantage of the new opportunities for enrichment, deepening social cleavages rather than filling them in. Wealthier and higher-achieving regions might try to separate themselves from poorer and lower-achieving ones, and distinctive homogeneous areas might try to acquire sovereignty—courses of action that might provoke violent responses from defenders of the status quo.

Of course, there are multiethnic societies in which ethnic consciousness remains weak, and even a more strongly developed sense of ethnicity may lead to political claims short of sovereignty. Sometimes, demands for ethnic autonomy or self-determination can be met within an existing state. The claims of the Catalans in Spain, the Flemish in Belgium, and the Scots in the United Kingdom have been met in this manner, at least for now. But such arrangements remain precarious and are subject to recurrent renegotiation. In the developing world, accordingly, where states are more recent creations and where the borders often cut across ethnic boundaries, there is likely to be further ethnic disaggregation and communal conflict. And as scholars such as Chaim Kaufmann have noted, once ethnic antagonism has crossed a certain threshold of violence, maintaining the rival groups within a single polity becomes far more difficult.

This unfortunate reality creates dilemmas for advocates of humanitarian intervention in such conflicts, because making and keeping peace between groups that have come to hate and fear one another is likely to require costly ongoing military missions rather than relatively cheap temporary ones. When communal violence escalates to ethnic cleansing, moreover, the return of large numbers of refugees to their place of origin after a cease-fire has been reached is often impractical and even undesirable, for it merely sets the stage for a further round of conflict down the road.

Partition may thus be the most humane lasting solution to such intense communal conflicts. It inevitably creates new flows of refugees, but at least it deals with the problem at issue. The challenge for the international community in such cases is to separate communities in the most humane manner possible: by aiding in transport, assuring citizenship rights in the new homeland, and providing financial aid for resettlement and economic absorption. The bill for all of this will be huge, but it will rarely be greater than the material costs of interjecting and maintaining a foreign military presence large enough to pacify the rival ethnic combatants or the moral cost of doing nothing.

Contemporary social scientists who write about nationalism tend to stress the contingent elements of group identity—the extent to which national consciousness is culturally and politically manufactured by ideologists and politicians. They regularly invoke Benedict Anderson's concept of "imagined communities, " as if demonstrating that nationalism is constructed will rob the concept of its power. It is true, of course, that ethnonational identity is never as natural or ineluctable as nationalists claim. Yet it would be a mistake to think that because nationalism is partly constructed it is therefore fragile or infinitely malleable. Ethnonationalism was not a chance detour in European history: it corresponds to some enduring propensities of the human spirit that are heightened by the process of modern state creation, it is a crucial source of both solidarity and enmity, and in one form or another, it will remain for many generations to come. One can only profit from facing it directly.

The Clash of Emotions

Fear, Humiliation, Hope, and the New World Order

Dominique Moïsi

JANUARY/FEBRUARY 2007

Thirteen years ago, Samuel Huntington argued that a "clash of civilizations" was about to dominate world politics, with culture, along with national interests and political ideology, becoming a geopolitical fault line ("The Clash of Civilizations?" Summer 1993). Events since then have proved Huntington's vision more right than wrong. Yet what has not been recognized sufficiently is that today the world faces what might be called a "clash of emotions" as well. The Western world displays a culture of fear, the Arab and Muslim worlds are trapped in a culture of humiliation, and much of Asia displays a culture of hope.

Instead of being united by their fears, the twin pillars of the West, the United States and Europe, are more often divided by them—or rather, divided by how best to confront or transcend them. The culture of humiliation, in contrast, helps unite the Muslim world around its most radical forces and has led to a culture of hatred. The chief beneficiaries of the deadly encounter between the forces of fear and the forces of humiliation are the bystanders in the culture of hope, who have been able to

DOMINIQUE MOÏSI is a Senior Adviser at the Institut Français des Relations Internationales (IFRI) in Paris.

concentrate on creating a better future for themselves.

These moods, of course, are not universal within each region, and there are some areas, such as Russia and parts of Latin America, that seem to display all of them simultaneously. But their dynamics and interactions will help shape the world for years to come.

THE CULTURE OF FEAR

The United States and Europe are divided by a common culture of fear. On both sides, one encounters, in varying degrees, a fear of the other, a fear of the future, and a fundamental anxiety about the loss of identity in an increasingly complex world.

In the case of Europe, there are layers of fear. There is the fear of being invaded by the poor, primarily from the South—a fear driven by demography and geography. Images of Africans being killed recently as they tried to scale barbed wire to enter a Spanish enclave in Morocco evoked images of another time not so long ago, when East Germans were shot at as they tried to reach freedom in the West. Back then, Germans were killed because they wanted to escape oppression. Today, Africans are being killed because they want to escape absolute poverty.

Europeans also fear being blown up by radical Islamists or being demographically conquered by them as their continent becomes a "Eurabia." After the bombings in Madrid in 2004 and London in 2005 and the scares this past summer, Europeans have started to face the hard reality that their homelands are not only targets for terrorists but also bases for them.

Then there is the fear of being left behind economically. For many Europeans, globalization has come to be equated with destabilization and job cuts. They are haunted by the fear that Europe will become a museum—a larger and more modern version of Venice, a place for tourists and retirees, no longer a center of creativity and influence.

Finally, there is the fear of being ruled by an outside power, even a friendly one (such as the United States) or a faceless one (such as the European Commission).

What unites all these fears is a sense of loss of control over one's territory, security, and identity—in short, one's destiny. Such concerns contributed to the no votes of the French and the Dutch last year on the referendum on the proposed EU constitution. They also explain the return of strong nationalist sentiments in many European countries—on display during the recent World Cup tournament.

Some of the same sense of loss of control is present in the United States. Although demographic fears are mitigated by the largely successful integration of Hispanics (compared with the difficulties surrounding the integration of Muslims in Europe), they are clearly present. The quarrel over the Spanish version of the American national anthem echoes the debate over the wearing of headscarves and veils in Europe.

Used to rates of growth significantly higher than those in most European countries, Americans do not fear economic decay the way Europeans do (although they worry about outsourcing). Yet they, too, are thinking of decline—in their bodies, with the plague of obesity; in their budgets, with the huge deficits; and in their spirit, with the loss of appetite for foreign adventures and a growing questioning of national purpose.

The United States' obsession with security after September 11 is understandable and legitimate. But what has it cost in terms of U.S. influence and image in the world? From the difficulties foreign travelers have entering U.S. territory to the human rights scandals of Guantánamo Bay, terrorists have at least in part succeeded in undermining the United States' claims of moral superiority and exceptionalism by prompting such reactions.

Whereas Europeans try to protect themselves from the world through a combination of escapism and appeasement,

Americans try to do so by dealing with the problem at its source abroad. But behind the Bush administration's forceful and optimistic rhetoric lies a somber reality, which is that the U.S. response to the September 11 attacks has made the United States more unpopular than ever. The U.S. intervention in Iraq, for example, has generated more problems than it has solved. Iraq is descending into civil war, and U.S. actions there have tipped the balance of power within the Muslim world to its most radical Shiite elements.

THE CULTURE OF HUMILIATION

Europeans started to reflect on their own decay after World War I: "We civilizations now know ourselves mortal," the French poet and philosopher Paul Valéry wrote in 1919. The Muslim world, meanwhile, has been obsessed with decay for centuries. When Europe was in its Middle Ages, Islam was at the peak of its Renaissance, but when the Western Renaissance started, Islam began its inexorable fall. From its defeat by a Christian fleet at the Battle of Lepanto, in 1571, to its failure to capture Vienna in 1683, to its final disappearance after World War I, the Ottoman Empire slowly shrank into oblivion.

The creation of the state of Israel in the midst of Arab land could only be seen by Muslims as the ultimate proof of their decay. For Jews, the legitimacy of Israel was manifold; it combined the accomplishment of a religious promise, the realization of a national destiny, and compensation by the international community for a unique crime, the Holocaust. For Arabs, by contrast, it was the anachronistic imposition of a Western colonial logic at the very moment decolonization was getting under way. In their view, crimes of the Christian West, fallen into barbarism against the Jews, were being unfairly paid for by the Muslim East.

The unresolved conflict between Israel and its neighbors has helped turn the culture of humiliation into a culture of hatred. Over time, the conflict's national character has shifted to its original religious basis—a conflict between Muslims and Jews, if not a clash between Islam and the West at large.

The combination of the deepening civil war in Iraq and the fighting in Lebanon between Hezbollah and Israel has reinforced a sense of outrage in many Muslims that has been fully exploited by Iran and its allies. In a war of images and symbols, Shiite extremists can appear to embody the spirit of resistance to humiliation, getting stronger with each blow they endure.

Globalization, meanwhile, has contributed to the problem. Every day, the Middle East is confronted with the contrast between globalization's winners, essentially the Western world and East Asia, and those who have been left behind.

The culture of humiliation is not limited to the Middle East but extends to the Muslim diaspora in the West as well. The riots that took place in France during the fall of 2005, for example, had an essentially socioeconomic origin, but they were also a lashing out by the disaffected against a society that claims to give them equal rights in principle but fails to do so in practice.

The gap is also, in part, the product of incompatible worldviews, stemming from different historical eras. As societies in Europe are becoming increasingly secular, the importance of religion in the daily life of the Muslim world is increasing. When Europeans look at Islam today, they are reminded of their own zealotry and wars of religion in the sixteenth and seventeenth centuries. This gap in mindset exists between the United States and the Muslim world as well, but it is less profound because the United States remains deeply religious and has even experienced a religious revival lately. Yet fundamentalism within Islam is unique in the sense that it is animated by a dual sense of revenge: by the Shiite minority against the Sunni majority and by the fundamentalists against the West at large.

Dominique Moïsi

THE CULTURE OF HOPE

As the West and the Middle East lock horns, confidence in progress has been moving eastward. An art exhibit displayed in 2005–6 at the Royal Academy of Arts, in London, entitled "China: The Three Emperors, 1662–1795," summarized new China's psychology. The explicit message of the exhibit, sponsored by Beijing, was clear: China is back. The central piece of the exhibit was a huge eighteenth-century painting, in the Jesuit-European style, showing the envoys of the West paying tribute to the Chinese emperor. After two centuries of relative decline, China is progressively recovering its legitimate international status. Its policy of concentrating on economic development while avoiding conflict seems to be working, earning Beijing both material benefits and international respect.

As for India, for the first time in its modern history it has stepped onto the world stage as both an independent and an important power. Cooperating diplomatically with the United States and making economic deals in Europe, the emerging Indian elites are displaying even more pride and optimism than their Chinese counterparts. The world's largest democracy will soon emerge as the most populous country, and it seems to know no limits.

Of course, Cassandras may rightly point out that strategic, economic, social, and political difficulties abound and that the culture of hope could easily collapse on itself like a house of cards. Asia has yet to witness the reconciliation between former enemies that constitutes the most remarkable achievement of postwar western Europe. The level of animosity in China and South Korea over Japan's treatment of the past evokes the situation of Europe in the 1950s. (China seems to have set double standards in this respect, never forgetting Japan's crimes while never remembering its own.) North Korea is a particularly dangerous rogue state. And arms races and nuclear proliferation in East Asia could set the region up for a terrible conflict down the road.

The gap that exists in China between the dynamism of the economy and the near incapacity or total reluctance of the present leadership to implement the most elementary and necessary political reforms does not bode well for the peaceful evolution of the country. Yet despite these concerns, there is hope among both leaders and publics across the region, and it seems likely to last as long as growth continues.

WHAT IS TO BE DONE?

In confronting this clash of emotions, the first priority for the West must be to recognize the nature of the threat that the Muslim world's culture of humiliation poses to Europe and the United States. Denying the threat's existence or responding to it in the wrong way are equally dangerous choices. Neither appeasement nor military solutions alone will suffice. The war that is unfolding is one that the culture of humiliation cannot win, but it is a war nonetheless and one that the West can lose by continuing to be divided or by betraying its liberal values and its respect for law and the individual. The challenge is not figuring out how to play moderate Islam against the forces of radicalism. It is figuring out how to instill a sufficient sense of hope and progress in Muslim societies so that despair and anger do not send the masses into the radicals' arms.

In that regard, the Israeli-Palestinian conflict appears more than ever as a microcosm of and possibly a precedent for what the world is becoming. Israel is the West, surrounded by the culture of humiliation and dreaming of escape from a dangerous region and of reentry into a culture of hope. But it must find a solution to the Palestinian problem first, or else the escape will not be possible. So, too, Europe and the United States seek to permanently banish their fears but will be able to do so only by finding a way to help the Muslim world solve its problems.

CPSIA information can be obtained at www.ICGtesting.com
Printed in the USA
LVOW10s0230260716

497776LV00013BA/58/P